Within the Realm of Happiness

Within the Realm of Happiness

Kinley Dorji

Produced by Siok Sian Pek-Dorji
Printed at Kuensel Corporation

CONTENTS

PREFACE

what is, not what should be

What do you think about when you are suspended in a moment of history... your own history? If it is an incredibly precious moment, like when you receive the Red Scarf from your King, you think about something practical, like not tripping over your sword and falling on your face.

The significance of the event itself hits you later, over the years.

It was December 9, 2006, the 20th day of the 10th month of the fire dog year. My family and I rushed home from Stanford University in California because I was awarded the Red Scarf. The trip was special. But what we did not know was that we were on the precipice of events so momentous that all our lives were to change.

I received my scarf in the morning and we learnt, that same day, that His Majesty King Jigme Singye Wangchuck, the fourth *Druk Gyalpo*, had handed over the reigns of governance to his son and heir, His Majesty Jigme Khesar Namgyal Wangchuck. The two Kings sat alone in the Throne room and made the sacred transition.

The father had achieved his destiny. The son would begin his.

The profundity of this gesture took some time to sink in. Our own lives being steeped in layers of man-made culture, it took time for us to understand that a transfer of the royal mantle could be so simple. We were blinded by the anticipation of the Coronation and the celebrations… in other words, our human expectations. Here was a new truth.

As the news spread, by word of mouth, Thimphu society went numb. Five days later it became official and the nation was in shock. As we discussed the news, in hushed tones, it struck me that His Majesty the King had taught us a supreme lesson in impermanence. The King was King no more. The rest of us suddenly found ourselves stripped of the petty images that we had built for ourselves. We were forced to ask, "Who are we? What are we?"

These powerful questions reminded me that I was a part of the intriguing phenomenon that is the human experience. I was a part of this complex web of interdependent life forms. I was living in a fascinating time in Bhutan's evolution. It was a privilege to be a part of it.

It also struck me that the stories of such overwhelming changes have to be told.

INTRODUCTION

in the land of the Thunder Dragon

Bhutan is one country that has had the good fortune of discovering itself. Hidden deep in the folds of the Himalayas the spectacular but formidable terrain kept the world out for centuries. Tiny village communities, scattered sparsely over the contours of the world's greatest mountain range, evolved with distinct cultures. In 1961, when the country decided it was ready to meet the world, it opened its doors, on its own terms. Today, having spanned centuries of what is believed to be human progress in five decades, Bhutan has arrived at yet another critical crossroad.

All nations grapple with change. For Bhutan this challenge has assumed a special significance as it negotiates the process of evolution. The Bhutanese experience is being increasingly viewed as an important experiment in interpreting the true value of progress. As human society strives to achieve well-being and happiness the world has seen, perhaps too frequently, what can go wrong. Is there a possibility that it can be done right?

from the blessings of the guardian deities

There is no record of Bhutan's early history before the eighth century and ancient Bhutan, therefore, is shrouded in blissful oblivion. Believed to have been inhabited since 2,000 BC, it was known as a fertile land where medicinal plants grew in abundance and where people lived in close harmony with nature. Geography decided the lifestyle of the people, with the terrain rising dramatically from sub tropical forests in the south, through temperate valleys, to the northern glaciers.

There was no concept of nationhood and borders. The terrain made communication difficult and small communities developed distinct cultural identities. The population of half a million people eventually developed four Bhutanese languages and 19 dialects. The people practiced forms of animism and the bon tradition that grew in Tibet and, over the years, became subsistence farmers.

Civilisation came with Buddhism. And the next stage of Bhutanese history, as chronicled in the scriptures, reads like mythology.

In the seventh century King Songtsen Gampo of Tibet placed Bhutan on the map of the Buddhist world when he built the Paro Kyichu Lhakhang and the Jambay Lhakhang in Bumthang, two of 108 monasteries as a part of a spiritual assignment. In the eighth century the deeply revered saint, Guru Rinpoche (Padmasambhava), sanctified the land and introduced Tantric Buddhism, the roots of Bhutanese culture.

Over the centuries that followed a number of Buddhist traditions were introduced. Phajo Drugom Zhigpo (1184-1251) introduced the Drukpa Kagyu school in the early 13th century. Terton Pema Lingpa (1450-1521), the great discoverer of spiritual treasures, revived the teachings of Guru Rinpoche. The outrageous holy rascal, Drukpa Kuenley (1455-1529), injected his earthy humour into the Bhutanese psyche.

Between 1616 and 1646 the dynamic Zhabdrung Ngawang Namgyel came from Tibet and integrated the scattered communities into a unified populace and established the concept of nationhood. A great master of the Drukpa Kagyu school the Zhabdrung crafted the distinctive dzongs and other infrastructure that accentuate the Bhutanese identity today. He strengthened Bhutan's cultural identity that has been preserved over the centuries. He also initiated a dual system of governance with the state clergy and temporal rulers sharing power until the beginning of the 20th century.

Thus Bhutan's historical heroes are enlightened beings who designed Bhutanese civilization. They are linked by prophesies and their vision ensured that Bhutan became the last bastion of Vajrayana Buddhism. Early forms of national governance was based on the tenets of Buddhism that provided administrative, moral, social and legal guidance. This process nurtured the mythological persona of the country even as Bhutan emerged as a modern nation state.

to the aura of kings

The 20th century was an extraordinary period for Bhutan. After decades of regional feuds, when the strong vied for power, and men were judged by the size of their calves, the Wangchuck dynasty consolidated national governance. Gongsar Ugyen Wangchuck was crowned as the first hereditary King on December 17, 1907. His ascension to the Throne ended a period of internal strife and launched an era of political stability. More important, it symbolised the transition of rule by physical strength to state-craft.

The Monarchy represented a shift into secular rule and the development of a modern economy. The relationship between the sovereign who bestowed benevolence and the people who submitted their devotion to the Monarch became the strength of Bhutan's political evolution. And the succession of hereditary Monarchs steered the country through rapid economic growth.

Bhutan made contact with the region which was then ruled by the British. Ugyen Wangchuck had good relations with the British and was an important mediator between the British and the Tibetan leadership. The second King, Jigme Wangchuck (1927-1952) strengthened Bhutan's relations with British India and with independent India. In 1949 Bhutan and India signed the treaty of friendship that has strongly influenced Bhutan's foreign policy. Ruling from his court in Bumthang, Jigme Wangchuck strengthened the rule of law, introduced a traditional education system, and developed a district administration system.

It was the third King, Jigme Dorji Wangchuck (1952-1972), who initiated the process of planned modernization. In 1961, soon after China took over Tibet, Bhutan shed centuries of self-imposed isolation and opened its doors to the world. Starting with basic infrastructure like roads and bridges, schools and hospitals, Bhutan launched itself into the development process, with most projects funded by the government of India.

The first generation of Bhutanese took up modern education both within and outside the country. Bhutan joined the United Nations in 1971. The third King set up the basis for modern governance with the structures for the separation of the different arms of government.

Modernisation and statecraft took on new meaning during the reign of the fourth King, Jigme Singye Wangchuck (1972-2006). After three extraordinary decades the kingdom of Bhutan moved into a new millennium as a testimony of political and economic success. The last country in South Asia to start planned development was earning the highest per capita income in the region by the end of the King's 34-year reign. This was achieved with a rich culture still intact, a much-appreciated pristine environment, and political initiatives that have startled the international community.

Scholars, intellectuals, development experts, even governments, believe today that Bhutan has provided a higher goal for development and change. The King's development philosophy of Gross National Happiness has forced the world to reflect deeply on the essence and purpose of human development.

The overriding characteristic of Bhutan's modernisation process is the sense of enlightenment with which the kingdom opened up to the world. By maintaining a fine blend of tradition and modernity the kingdom was able to achieve phenomenal progress without losing its mystical aura. The inner values of the Bhutanese identity that enabled Bhutan to flourish over the centuries remained the basis of change. This was the essence of the legacy that King Jigme Singye Wangchuck handed over to the fifth King, Jigme Khesar Namgyal Wangchuck.

to the good fortunes of the people

Exactly 100 years later, the Kings handed over the power of governance to the people. On December 9, 2006, Jigme Khesar Namgyal Wangchuck, the heir to the Golden Throne, took over the helm as head of state. In this historic transition, the fifth Druk Gyalpo inherited the responsibility to institute the country's first democratically elected government.

In the interpretation of the Bhutanese psyche the authority and responsibility of governance has been "bestowed" on the people. The Monarch has stepped back and the government is elected through adult franchise. While the Kings of Bhutan will be a safety net in the foreseeable future, the will of the citizens will reside in an elected parliament.

This is the crossroad that Bhutan straddles today, looking back at a mythology that unraveled to form a unique kingdom, and forward at a future that represents a thrilling challenge. The challenge is foreboding because change is not initiated for the sake of change but with the mandate that change has to be for the better. The dilemma for the Bhutanese people, and the new leadership, is to continue the extraordinary successes of the past. As the fifth King of Bhutan pledged in his first address to the nation on December 17, 2006:

"The country that is before us, the country that we see and know, the country that has been handed to us, is the country which His Majesty built through his selfless service... His Majesty has placed his full trust in us and we the people must fulfill his vision and our own duty to future generations of Bhutanese... I share His Majesty's complete faith in the people and I believe that we will, as His Majesty has bestowed today, leave to our own children such a gift in 30 years."

Bhutan looks around the world, at emerging, struggling, and failed democracies, and sees much to be feared. Evolution succeeds, not just through vision and dreams, but only when it is practical and applicable. Political transformation, therefore, must suit the people. And, at the same time, the populace must be ready to earn its benefits.

Bhutanese society is under more pressure than ever before. The forces of globalisation, the invasion of commercial media, the complex implications of development and progress are tugging at the roots of the traditional values system that kept the society intact for centuries. The collective merit earned by decades of spiritual practice and honest hard work is threatened by the forces of materialism.

The lifestyle of the people is changing as a subsistence farming society, still strong on the oral tradition, is caught in the urban drift. The traditional social system and values break down under the powerful forces of change. The real challenge is that Bhutan must control change and not be controlled by change.

to Gross National Happiness

Bhutan's answer to change lies in the wisdom of Gross National Happiness. This philosophy provides the wisdom with which the past speaks to the future through the present. King Jigme Khesar Namgyal Wanghuck, now seen as the guardian of GNH, tells the people that Gross National Happiness must become a "national consciousness". And, while the GNH vision of the past was intuitive wisdom, Bhutanese intellectuals are constructing its academic base for the future.

Bhutan will never be a military power or an economic force. Its strength lies in the moral principles that have given this small kingdom the large ideals that Gross National Happiness represents. Having dared to be different, and having presented the world with higher goals for human progress, Bhutan must now make it work at home. As King Jigme Khesar Namgyal Wangchuck told the people when he took the helm in 2006, failure is not an option.

ANGAY

The mouse stopped about two feet from the ball of rice and eyed it, not with the cunning of a predator, but with what looked to me like strategically feigned innocence. It moved closer, waited for a while, its eyes darting around the room, and then scurried around the small wooden board on which my grandmother had placed the rice ball. I tensed under my warm yak-hair quilt as the furry gray figure climbed nimbly on the board and walked towards the bait.

***

It was the winter of 1968. I was 10 years old. I remember the year because I had fallen off the roof of our cowshed where I was playing and cracked the shinbones on both legs. The traditional healer had given me a cup of *ara* as a painkiller and "fitted" the bones back together with his hands while my father held me to stop me from struggling. My mother ran outside so she couldn't hear me screaming.

Three months later the pain was gone, the wooden splint removed, and I had started walking. But I was still allowed to sleep with my grandmother, Angay Tomu, near the hearth in the kitchen. It was the warmest part of the house because of the embers that stayed alive all night and the fire that she would start before dawn to cook the morning broth.

***

Angay Tomu had designed the mousetrap herself. Every night she placed a ball of rice on a wooden board that was about two feet long, one foot wide, and an inch thick. She placed over it, face down, an old clay pot about 10 inches in diameter at the rim. Then she lifted one side of the pot to an angle of 45 degrees and balanced it on a thin six-inch long stick. The concept was that, in the process of picking up the rice ball, the mouse would somehow knock the stick out of the way, and the pot would slam down, trapping it inside.

I woke up before dawn every morning to watch the fascinating game between Angay Tomu and the mouse. It had been going on for about three weeks. The mouse, about six inches long from its nose to the tip of its tail, would come out after the fire was lit so it could see the rice ball in the glow of the flames. After skirting the trap, sometimes until the first rays of the sun came in through the small window above the hearth, it would walk stealthily to the rice ball, not touching the stick or the pot, pick it up in its small jaws and scurry away.

Outside, frost covered the ground like a gray blanket in the pre-dawn light.

***

Angay Tomu was about five feet tall, dressed in the dark red *anim's* (nun) dress that Bhutanese women change into permanently after they "retired" from farm work and began full time Buddhist practice to gain merit for the next life. Her close-cropped gray hair was always covered with a red cap. It had flaps that she lowered in winter to keep her ears warm. I had never seen her wrinkled face unruffled as she chanted her prayers from dawn to dusk – *Om Mane Padme Hum* - repeating it fast so it sounded like she was humming under her breath.

She showed none of the frustration that I began to feel, although the mouse had now eaten 16 of her rice balls. In fact she and the mouse appeared to ignore each other. She would place a new ball of rice every evening and seemed completely unaware of the little creature as she stoked the coals into a fire by placing some resin-coated blue pine shavings on the coal and blowing on them to coax the first flames. Its eyes on the rice ball, the mouse was equally unperturbed even when Angay nearly stepped on its tail as she walked around the room doing her chores.

***

Then it happened.

The mouse picked up the rice ball and, as it was walking past the stick it turned around, for some reason, to look at Angay who was bent over the hearth, chanting and stirring the pot of rice broth. As it turned back to run away, with the rice ball in its mouth, the mouse stumbled, fell against the stick, and the pot came down with a thump. It was trapped.

The tension that had built in me over three weeks made me leap up, shouting, "Angay, Angay, it's caught. The mouse is in the pot." Angay continued stirring her pot, not even looking at the trap. My parents, irritated to be woken up at dawn, did not share my excitement so I ran, barefoot on the frost, to my aunt's house next door to announce the news. My three-year old cousin wanted to see the mouse but the adults showed no interest.

***

Breakfast was agonisingly slow. I couldn't take my eyes off the round bottom of the inverted pot as I ate the steaming broth. I wondered what the mouse was doing inside. I understood that it would now stop making holes in our rice bags in the store but I wanted to know what Angay was going to do with it.

After breakfast Angay Tomu packed some dry puffed rice in a small cane basket which she tucked into the front fold of her dress. This was her favourite snack and it meant that she was planning a journey.

She picked up the wooden board, making sure that the pot did not move, and placed it on her head. She walked through the village and crossed the glacial stream that ran along the edge of the village, stepping cautiously on the tree trunk that served as a crude bridge. Then, following the woodcutters' path into the forest, she walked for two hours, holding the board with one hand, her feet making a crackling sound on the dry oak leaves.

Angay Tomu stopped deep in the forest, choosing a spot where the acorns lay thick on the ground and a swift little brook kept the area green. A number of small creatures darted among the raspberry bushes, dandelion flowers, and prickly shrubs that grew on both sides of the stream. She carefully lowered the board and placed it on the ground. She knelt down beside it and lifted the pot. The mouse scurried away and disappeared into the bushes.

29

MI-MI'S SURPRISE

"Mi-mi, tell us how Drukpa Kuenley made the robber boss eat his shit."

Mi-mi's (grandfather) face crinkles into a grin. He has told the story more than 20 times but the children are not bored with it. Neither is he tired of telling the story. The fire from the hearth accentuates the shadows on his face as he assumes an exaggeratedly thoughtful look, as if he is trying to remember the story.

He clears his throat. "Now, Drukpa Kuenley…"

His audience is tense as Mi-mi builds the suspense to the point where the gang of robbers stop in the forest to open the leather pouch that they have stolen from Drukpa Kuenley as he lay sleeping in a cave. They do not know that Drukpa Kuenley already knew, by premonition, that they were going to rob him. He has emptied his money pouch, defecated in it, and left it near his bedroll while he pretended to be asleep. When the gang leader dips his hand into the faeces he shouts "akayee" and flings his hand downwards to get the faeces off his fingers. His knuckles hit a stone on the ground and, in the agony of the moment, he impulsively puts his knuckles in his mouth to ease the pain.

By then the entire family is in fits of laughter. Eight-year old Dorji is rolling on the floor holding his stomach. This happens every time.

***

Like all other families in the village Dorji's family starts eating dinner soon after sunset. Everyone sits cross-legged on the floor, around the two large pots from which his mother serves the rice and *ema datshi* (chilli and cheese). The long red chillis from the garden in front of the house are cooked into a gluey mix in fresh home-made cheese. Dorji's grandparents, then his father, and then his younger brother and sister pass their *bangchus* (cane baskets used as plates) and cups to her and she fills them, medium portions for the grandparents, a large portion for his father, and more gravy than chillis for the children.

The room serves as both dining room and kitchen. In winter the kerosene lantern is lit early because it is completely dark by the time they finish the meal. The fire in the hearth in the corner of the room is kept alive, both for its warmth and light, with Mi-mi sitting close to it. After dinner Dorji's father mashes fermented millet in a small copper pot. He pours hot water into it, mixes it well, then pushes a small basket into the pot. As the warm drink is strained into the basket he uses a ladle to pour some for himself and Mi-mi. On winter evenings his mother and grandmother also drink a small cup each.

This is the best time for stories. The adults take turns telling stories but it is usually Mi-mi who keeps everyone rapt, his stories becoming more interesting as he gets more animated. "They are too young for this," says Dorji's mother one night when he started a story of how Drukpa Kuenley tamed a demoness with his massive penis. "Why not?" says Mi-mi. "Its better that they learn from me than from someone else."

***

One night Mi-mi has just begun his story when Miktshe, the large black mastiff who is tied outside the house, starts barking, a signal that someone is approaching the house. Moments later the heavy front door creaks open. Sonam, Dorji's 10-year old cousin, walks in. She switches off her torch, takes out the two batteries, and places them on the warm pot that is sitting on the hearth. The torchlight is brighter when the batteries are warm. New batteries are hard to come by.

"My father sent me to tell you that he saw a jungle cat caught in a noose in your fence, near the old willow tree," says Sonam. "He says it's a big cat. It's dead."

For a while everyone is silent. Wild cats are not popular in the village because they steal chickens from the farms but everyone knows that you chase them away, not kill them. Dorji's father says that if you kill an animal you will be born as that animal in your next life and the animal will be born as you and it will kill you.

"I knew that Singye was up to something," says Dorji's father. "I saw him near the fence this afternoon."

"The poor boy," says Dorji's grandmother. "Imagine the bad karma."

***

Dorji keeps his head down. His ears feel hot as they usually do when he is uncomfortable. Singye is his friend, a 14-year old boy who lives alone with his mother on the edge of the village. They have no land so he usually works on his neighbours' fields to support his mother. In his spare time he goes out into the forest to collect wild orchids called *ola chhoto* because they look like a crow's beak. Dorji has accompanied Singye to the motor road where he waits for passing vehicles and stops them to sell the orchids, a very popular delicacy.

Singye occasionally traps wild pheasants to eat. Dorji has been out in the forests with Singye. In fact he found it very exciting to help Singye set traps. The idea is to build a fence of thickly woven branches, as dense as a hedge, that cuts off an area where the pheasants like to feed. Then you make a small hole in the hedge, through which a bird can run, and hang the noose, made of strong twine, around the circumference of the hole. The other end of the noose is tied firmly to a nearby sapling.

When the birds go to feed they have to go through the fence. The first bird that tries to squeeze through the gap in the fence gets caught in the noose. The noose tightens and throttles the bird when it thrashes about in panic. Singye says that his father used to set several traps along one fence and catch two or three pheasants at one time.

***

Dorji knew that Singye had set a trap in the fence that afternoon. He was hoping to catch the pheasants that were sure to come from the forest to eat the wheat seeds that had just been sown. The cat had obviously tried to squeeze through the gap.

He does not tell his father that he knew about the trap. Like last week he did not tell his parents that he had taken some rice and cooking oil from the house, as Singye asked him, so they could cook a rice and pheasant curry picnic in the forest. He did not enjoy what he had thought would be a great adventure because Singye had invited a girl from the village and the two of them had ignored Dorji throughout the picnic.

∗∗∗

Dorji can't breathe. Every time he moves the noose around his neck gets tighter. He can't move his hands so he thrashes his legs about. Some dark faces are laughing at him.

"Wake up, Dorji, let's go for a walk." Dorji wakes up with a start, relieved to find out that it was just a dream.

It is dawn. Instead of sitting in his bedroll chanting his prayers Mi-mi, fully dressed with a woollen scarf around his head, is shaking Dorji awake. Dorji gets up and quickly wraps his *gho* around him. Mi-mi helps him get dressed. He doesn't ask where they are going because he knows that when Mi-mi asks him to go somewhere it is always with good reason. And it is usually fun.

Outside the house Mi-mi gestures for Dorji to walk ahead. "Show me where the trap is." That is Mi-mi. He knows that Dorji knew about the trap all along.

***

The hedge around the trap is broken and uprooted from the last desperate throes of the animal. The cat is lying on its side, its twisted head entangled in the hedge. To Dorji it looks like a very large cat or a young leopard cub. The fur is mostly light gray with a snow white patch at the throat. It has dark spots scattered over the body. Dorji feels a sense of awe looking at this animal which was, just yesterday, a swift and elegant predator. He likes to watch cats move because they are so graceful. This one must have been powerful. He reaches out to feel the thick soft fur as Mimi pulls out an eight-inch knife out of his *gho* and cuts the noose.

The body of the jungle cat in an old sack flung over Mi-mi's shoulder, they head home. They walk in silence for some time.

"Mi-mi, do you think the jungle cat's spirit might take revenge on me because I knew about the trap?" This thought has been bugging him.

"No. We say such things because we want to teach young people to think very seriously before they kill animals. You did not mean

39

to harm the cat."

After some time Mi-mi adds: "Dorji, it is okay for you to be interested in things like traps because you have to learn the ways of the forest."

They walk on. "We live in a land of forests so sometimes we are forced to kill. When I was young I had to hunt and fish if I wanted to eat meat. Sometimes we even have to kill to protect ourselves. But you must not kill anything, not even a fly, without a very good reason."

***

Mi-mi goes to work as soon as he gets home. He sharpens his all-purpose knife on a wet stone. As Dorji, an eager assistant, holds the front paws apart, Mi-mi makes a neat cut at the throat and slices the skin down the stomach to its tail. Dorji holds the animal in different positions as Mi-mi slices through the transparent fascia very carefully to separate the skin from the muscle without damaging the skin.

Once the skin is stripped off the body of the animal Mi-mi takes it to the run-off water canal that runs down the front of house to the paddy fields. He immerses the skin, stretched flat, in the water and places a stone on it to hold it below the surface. He keeps it in the water five days to soften it.

On the sixth morning Mi-mi takes the skin out and cleans it, scraping out little bits of flesh and fascia with his knife. Then Dorji holds the skin flat on the ground and Mi-mi drives wooden pegs through the paws, tail, and neck so it is stretched taut in the sun, the inside facing up. Dorji is assigned the responsibility, for the next three days, to protect the skin from stray dogs that linger in the vicinity. The lean and hungry strays come every morning when the skin is stretched out and hover around until it is taken into the cellar at night.

A week later the skin is dry and Mi-mi goes to work softening it. He dabs thick mustard oil on the inside of the skin and kneads it between his bare feet. He places the skin on a wooden board near the outside wall of the house and, leaning his hands against the wall, he stomps on it for an hour or so, turns it around, and kneads it again.

"Mi-mi, what are you making?" Dorji asks every day.

"You'll see," Mi-mi answers every day.

***

One day Mi-mi takes Dorji to the next village, about two hours'

41

walk through the dense forest of Oak and Rhododendron trees. They go to the house of the famed saddlebag maker, Ap Norbu, and Mi-mi trades three *dre* (measuring bowl) of rice for a large steel needle and a ball of thread made out of nettle fibre. Used for stitching hide, it is called a *ta-khap* (horse needle), probably because it is larger than the needles that tailors use.

On the way back they find a sunny spot near a stream to eat their packed lunch of rice and chunks of pork cooked in chilli. Mi-mi swigs some *chhang* (rice wine) from his flask and burps with great satisfaction while Dorji drinks fresh water from the clear brook. He has learnt not to put his mouth in the water, as he would like to do, because a leech could get into his nose. He cups the water in his hands and brings it up to his mouth.

Although the forest is filled with wild animals Dorji is not frightened when he is with Mi-mi. They often stop to cut fine bamboo reeds that grow near the streams and, collecting feathers dropped by pheasants, Mi-mi makes arrows for Dorji and his friends. Mi-mi has taught him to recognise edible mushrooms and to avoid the poisonous varieties. Mi-mi can make flutes out of bamboo reeds and play beautiful tunes. He tells Dorji to whistle or sing when he walks through the forest so that the wild animals will hear him and move away. A wild animal will never attack a person unless it is frightened by the person and this happens when they come upon each other unexpectedly.

Mi-mi is busy during the day, taking the cows out to graze or collecting firewood and water from the common source that the villagers share. He works on the skin in the mornings before breakfast and evenings before it gets completely dark.

He draws lines on the inside of the skin with a piece of charcoal, using his thumb and fingers as measuring tools. Then he takes great pains to cut the skin with his knife. He calls Dorji to thread the nettle fibre through the needle, because his own eyesight is not so good, and begins stitching the skin, undoing and re-stitching it many times until he is satisfied.

***

It is soon the middle of February and Dorji has to return to boarding school in northern India. The morning after the full moon Dorji's father straps two bags of rice on the mule which he has hired from his cousin's family. He will sell the rice in Thimphu and buy Dorji's shoes and socks, soap, toothbrush, and toothpaste. Dorji carries a small bag of puffed rice that his mother has made.

Mi-mi walks with them for several hours on the first day until they stop for lunch. "You must study hard and be first in class," says Mi-mi after lunch. "But you must not forget the forest which is our home." Then he pulls out of his *gho* pocket a beautiful fur cap, made from the skin of the jungle cat, and gives it to Dorji. It is a round cap with a peak in front to shade his eyes. It has flaps on the two sides, tied together at the top. They can be untied and lowered so that the soft fur covers his ears in winter.

Dorji's face breaks into a happy grin. He puts on the cap and turns around to follow his father who is leading the mule down the hill, the bell around its neck tinkling as it negotiates the winding track. Mi-mi's face crinkles into a smile as he watches his grandson walk disappear into the distance, the cap bobbing up and down as he walks fast to keep up with his father's longer strides.

Two Men, Two Worlds

"Oy apa, are you going up?"

It is a typical Bhutanese greeting. The man is walking uphill. If the man had been walking downhill he would be asked "Are you going down?" In Bhutan when you see someone leave you ask "Are you leaving?" If someone is eating you ask "Are you eating?" It is common that when you meet someone you ask "Are you here?"

It is the understatement that says nothing, and everything. The answer you expect, and usually receive, is "Yes." The question often means nothing more than an acknowledgement of another human being in the vicinity. Sometimes it represents a lot more. "Have you arrived?" could be an expression of the profound emotions of a mother greeting her child who has been away for a year in boarding school.

★

It is the year 2000 and this tradition is becoming less pronounced, particularly among the growing urban population. Battered by the process that the world calls development, which would imply that life is getting better, people have less inclination for small talk. Some would say that it is because Bhutanese life is moving at a faster pace and people have no time. Others would say that people are becoming less humane.

But up here on Sangye-Gang, high above Thimphu city, the prayer flags still flutter along the ridge, the wind still whispers through the pine needles, and the air is still clean. The concrete jungle of the capital sits in the valley far below. It is natural for one man, in his mid-40s to greet another man, about the same age, with no specific reason.

★

The sun is setting. The speaker, in a black Nike jogging suit and Air Nike running shoes, bends over in a classic exercise to stretch his back muscles. Then, with his hands supporting his lower back, he bends backwards 45-degrees.

The other man is wearing an old woolen *mathra gho* under which a pair of faded blue track pants is tucked into his knee-length green socks. He has just stepped on to the black-tarred road, having climbed up the almost vertical footpath. Both are panting slightly.

***

"Yes," says the man in the *gho*. "I'm going up."

Then, perhaps because they are the only two people on the hill, or perhaps because he is not in a hurry, or perhaps his mood is buoyed by a drink or two, he adds: "I had run out of matches so I went down to buy some."

With no other houses "up" in that direction the man must live on the Phajoding ridge. The Phajoding monastery houses a *shaydra*, a tertiary institute for monks who have reached the level of Buddhist studies when they are expected to go into a three-year meditation retreat. It is a two-to-four hour walk, depending on how fit a person is. For tourists a visit to the monastery is a day trip.

"You don't have a car?" asks the man in the *gho*, not seeing any parked nearby. He knows that people who dress like this usually have cars. There are so many cars in Thimphu there is no space to walk these days. These people even drive their cars to buy vegetables.

"No, I came here to get some exercise," says the man in the tracksuit. "You know we drive to work, sit in an office all day, and drive home so we get no exercise."

He was testing a new pair of running shoes that is supposed to absorb the jar on paved surfaces. It is necessary on the Motithang hill, particularly for the steep descent, where cars have to drive on first gear. His son, who spends all his spare time surfing the Internet told him that Nike was now installing a speedometer in the sole of a new shoe model so that the owner can check the distance he walks. It will have a wireless connection so he can even check his speed on an Ipod.

**

The man in the *gho* wears green canvas shoes that have been imported from China for Nu. 90.00 a pair. Bhutan's trade with the fastest growing economy on earth is conducted on the back of mules, with smugglers sleeping during the day and traveling at night across the Tibetan border. The shoes are purely symbolic for this man because the soles of his bare feet, that have walked hundreds of kilometres of hard ground, are tougher than the plastic soles. The large toe of his left foot sticks out of a gap where the glue sticking canvas and sole has given way.

***

The man in the *gho*, who walks down to the city every week to buy groceries, sees a growing number of people walking on this quiet road these days. He sees older men and women toiling up the hill with prayer beads in hand, some young women in very tight pants that were shocking and seductive, and young men in jogging suits. He sees ministers walking with their bodyguards, aums with their maids, and families with their dogs.

He himself walks at least a few hours every day but for different reasons. He has to take his herd of three cows and one bull to graze in the morning and bring them home in the evening, he has to fetch firewood from the forest, and drinking water from the nearby stream. Once or twice a week he has to walk to the market for errands or to the gup's office for paper work. He has walked all his life.

He would like to change places with any of these people. Then they could get their exercise and he could drive their cars.

***

More recently the man in the *gho* sees groups of young boys rub the oil off the cannabis plants that grow all over the hillside, mix it with cigarettes, and smoke them under the parapets along the road or behind the cover of the trees. He sees them getting intoxicated and giggling senselessly for hours. It puzzles him and he wishes that they would at least do it on the road where there is less danger of setting the forest on fire. Thimphu is filled with bars and these boys are consuming this plant which is used as pig fodder. He himself prefers *ara*.

What makes him a little nostalgic is when young boys and girls walk into the forests in the evenings and thrash about on the soft pine needles. The best memories of his own youth, herding cows and fetching firewood in the forest, are when he used to wait for the neighbourhood girls to come into the forest to collect fodder for their cows and pigs. He will never forget the afternoon when Om, the prettiest girl in the village, let him lift her *kira* all the way up. They used to sing together when the cows grazed.

After three years Om left him for a clerk in the district office. He saw her recently in Thimphu city, with powder on her cheeks and red lipstick, riding on the back of a green scooter. She pretended that she did not know him.

***

Impulsively, it appears, the man in the *gho* reaches into his *hemchu* (front fold of the *gho*), takes out a bottle of Golden Eagle beer and offers it to the man in the jogging suit. It is a gesture of hospitality that has been nurtured through generations of people. He has learned from his parents that "you do not let people leave your home with an empty stomach and that acquaintances should not part empty-handed".

To the jogger the bottle of the worst beer ever produced by man, held out to him by a pair of rough hands, suddenly seems worth more than all the imported spirits in his cabinet or the imported beer cans in his refrigerator. The exchange of gifts that was an accepted social norm in the past now carries the connotations of bribery in modern society. Today people seem to offer gifts only when they want something.

"Thank you. But you deserve that more than me." He means it.

"It's a long way to come to buy matches," he adds. "How is life up there?"

The man in the *gho* squints up towards the ridge, now bathed in the soft sunset. The light plays on the layer of snow dusting, reflecting an orange glow. He looks down at the city sprawled below them. There is a thickening layer of smog forming, a mixture of the dull gray fumes of diesel engine cars and the blue smoke that spirals up from the wood stove chimneys. "I do not have an education," he says, in a tone suggesting modesty more than regret. "So this simple life is all I deserve."

"Will it snow this year?" The two men look up, instinctively, at the Phajoding ridge. Beyond the ridge lie three glacial lakes, deeply revered by the older generation of Bhutanese and loved by the youth as scenic camping spots.

"I hope so," says the man in the *gho*. "It did not snow last year. It used to snow every year in Thimphu, at least once or twice. It is not a good omen when it does not snow. It means that the guardian deities are not happy."

That makes sense to the jogger. Bhutan sees an all-round drop in water volume when it does not snow in winter. Without snow on the mountain peaks the clear blue mountain streams go dry. That means there is not enough water to irrigate the paddy fields or to turn the hydropower turbines. And it is not just Bhutan. There is plenty of evidence now of the ecological balance being upset around the world as man encroaches on to nature. The wrath of the deities is not so mysterious.

✳✳✳

"Do you like coming down to the city?"

"No." The response is spontaneous. "Last month my bull broke loose from his harness and ran away from his shed. I searched for him for 11 hours and eventually found him in the city, outside a dasho's gate. "The aum scolded me and told me that it had eaten her flowers. She said they cost thousands of Ngultrum in foreign countries. The next time it happened she said that she would put me in jail."

"We try to avoid the city".

A man and his bull, aliens in what was once their land.

***

It is getting dark. The jogger hopes that the archers down the road have finished for the day. It is another example of how Bhutanese officialdom does not know how to deal with a changing society. The archers have changed their soft bamboo bows and arrows for powerful compound bows and aluminium arrows and shoot across the road, endangering people who are walking. The city corporation says it's the forestry department's responsibility to establish rules of safety, the forestry department says it is within the urban boundary, the department of urban development blames the sports authorities, and the archery federation says it has nothing to do with the rules beyond the national competitions. So nobody makes a decision.

The same with cars. The five-kilometre road from Thimphu city to Sangye-Gang is a popular spot for people learning to drive and there are more new learners every day. Bhutanese officials make long speeches on preserving the environment but keep passing policies that suffocate the air. More cars are becoming available, banks are offering a greater variety of loans, and there are no rules on the proportion of the number of cars to the road length. Deteriorating engines release dense clouds of diesel smoke into the atmosphere.

He flexes his knees and starts jogging, down into the valley where the people are beginning to shut their doors against the evening breeze and noisy neighbours.

***

The man in the *gho*, who has been standing on the edge of the road where he climbed up, starts walking up the hill in easy, measured steps. The sun has dropped behind the high ridge, throwing the dwarf Rhododendron trees into the shade. He has bought his box of matches but still needs the firewood to cook his evening meal and he has to collect that from the forest before it gets completely dark.

Regrettably the trees are losing all their branches and the forest line is receding. With so much construction activity in the city thousands of workers go into the forest at night and cut off the branches for firewood. When the forest guards were allowed to keep the fines they used to be more active stopping people collecting firewood illegally. They stopped patrolling the forests when the rule was stopped.

***

It is not likely that the two men will meet again. They live in the same valley but not in the same world.

PRETTY WOMAN

The village

The young woman is bent almost double, vigorously soaping her hair, face, shoulders, and neck. Her faded blue flannel petticoat is pulled up so the elastic holds it just below her breasts. It is wrapped around her buttocks and thighs with the end bunched together and held between her knees. She is singing as she rubs the somewhat hard cake of red Lifebuoy soap with some effort to work up a lather.

The water, a natural spring, flows down the mountain into the village which is a scenic sprawl of terraced fields that are cut into the steep slopes. The foot-wide community canal meanders down through the terraces taking the spring water past the houses. As the water flows past each house it is tapped with a *zaa*, a three or four-foot hollow half log that channels a small jet of water towards the house. It is a continuously-flowing tap, shared by the people and domestic animals, and the drain-off waters the vegetable gardens.

The 12 houses in the village are spread out. Each house has its own space, surrounded by clumps of trees, bamboo, and vegetable gardens. Beside every house is a cowshed and a pig sty and some have chicken coops. Multi-coloured hens, mostly with red, brown, and white feathers, and the occasional rooster clucks around the houses during the day, pecking titbits from the ground. Most families keep a fierce guard dog to warn them of leopards that come to steal hens. These mastiffs are usually locked in a strong wooden house to stop them from biting visitors and to protect them from the leopards.

***

Bent forward to catch the stream of water before it hits the drain, the woman does not see 10-year old Kuenley who runs down the slope along the canal. Ignoring the twisting path, he nimbly dodges artemesia and cannabis bushes and clumps of bamboo, and jumps over a variety of dwarf shrubs, some of them with serrated leaves that have sharp thorns sticking out of them. Puffs of dust rise as his bare feet hit the dry earth. He clears the last patch of yellowish green shrubs with a leap, landing near the woman.

"Ow Thrimi," says Kuenley. "My mother sent me to borrow your *dre* (measuring bowl)."

Rubbing a new layer of soap into her closely cropped hair, she does not hear him.

"Ow Thrimi!" Kuenley shouts.

Still bent over, Thrimi stops and turns her head sideways to look at Kuenley. She squints through the soap bubbles that make her eyes smart.

"Oy Kuenley," she says. "Wait, I can't hear you."

She places the soap on a flat piece of stone on the edge of the canal and moves forward, placing her head under the stream of water to rinse the soap off. When she is satisfied that the soap is all gone she runs her fingers through her hair and straightens up to face Kuenley. Her neck, rounded shoulders, and muscled arms are burned dark brown. Her large and firm breasts are much fairer. The water trickles from her hair and face, down her arms, between her breasts.

"What did you say?"

"My mother wants to borrow your *dre*. The trader from Thinleygang has come to collect the rice that we owe him and uncle Tashi has taken our *dre* to Thimphu. He's gone to sell some rice at the weekend market."

"Let me finish washing," says Thrimi. She lifts her petticoat higher up her thighs and sticks out her legs, one at a time, under the jet of water. She soaps her sturdy thighs and calves and rinses them. Then she soaps her feet and uses a small flat stone to scrape the hardened skin around the edges of her feet. The skin on her heels are cracked and the soles of her feet coarse from years of outdoor life without shoes.

***

Kuenley likes Thrimi, with her red cheeks and bright eyes and ready smile. She is known to be the prettiest woman in the village. She is the best singer and the centre of attention at village festivals. Twenty years old, she is also admired for her strength as she goes about the seasonal chores of a village woman. In winter she carries home loads of firewood for the house, dry oak leaves for her cowshed, and takes baskets of manure out to the fields. In spring she plants the chillis and spinach in the garden in front of the house and radish and turnips behind the house. In summer she is out in the rice fields transplanting the seedlings as her uncle ploughs the ground. In autumn she has to harvest, thresh, and mill the rice.

Thrimi picks up a small gray cotton towel sitting on the ground and quickly wipes her face, neck, breasts and stomach. "Come," she says. Throwing the towel around her neck so the two ends cover her breasts, she picks up the soap with her left forefinger and thumb and walks to the wooden ladder that goes up to the outdoor deck that leads into the house. She climbs the near-vertical ladder with ease, ignoring the handrail that runs on her right, her back muscles rippling gently on both sides of the spine.

Kuenley follows her up to the deck and through the large open door into the house. The spacious all-purpose room has a neat mud hearth against one wall and a double-deck window on the other. An array of pots and pans sit on two rows of shelves above the hearth. The only furniture in the room is a wooden box against the wall beside the hearth, the rice container. Some ropes and tools hang on wooden pegs near the door. Thrimi unhooks the *dre* which is hanging by a thin leather strap above the rice box and hands it to him. "We need it back tomorrow."

Kuenley glances at the man in a black *gho* sitting cross-legged on a black bear-skin rug near the open window, his back to the room. He is using the late-morning sunlight to see better as he turns and twists strands of dry nettle bark into a rope. His head is cocked a little to the right so he can use his good eye. Kuenley knows Thrimi's uncle, Dom Saymi (bear killer).

***

All the boys in the village are in awe of Dom Saymi who got his name because he killed a bear with his *dozom*, a double-edged 18-inch knife that tapers evenly into a sharp point. The *dozom* is a multi-purpose tool that every man, and some women, carry, tucked diagonally into their belts in front. The story is that Dom Saymi and the Himalayan Black Bear suddenly came upon each other on a narrow path above the village. The bear sprang on him as wild animals do when they are surprised. As they wrestled over the bushes Dom Saymi pulled out his *dozom* and stabbed the bear repeatedly in the stomach until it collapsed on him. The bear had ripped off the left side of Dom Saymi's face, including his left eye and nose.

He does not talk because his mouth is disfigured. He works on the farm and makes nettle ropes that the farmers use to tie their oxen and cows in their sheds at night, to carry firewood, and for other necessities. Thrimi lives with him, her father having left the village with another woman when she was 10 years old and her mother having died of a stomach disease when she was 15 years old.

Kuenley bounds down the steps and runs up the path towards his house. He bumps into Nado, who suddenly jumps out from behind a thick Rhododendron bush. Nado is an 18-year old cowherd who helps his parents look after 17 cows belonging to the monk body. They live on the edge of the village and graze the cows in the community forest. "Isn't she pretty?" asked Nado. "Did you look at her breasts? I couldn't see them too clearly from here because she was bent down most of the time."

"Yes," said Kuenley, who had not looked at her breasts. It seemed the right thing to say to an older boy who had been hiding in the bushes peeping at Thrimi washing.

***

The dancing picks up pace. Four men and two women started at an easy gait, singing a pleasant folk song, and maintaining the rhythm with their steps, as they moved in a circle around the bonfire. Other men and women join as they get inspired by the songs and as they drink enough to find the courage. By the third song eight men and five women are stomping in unison, singing a little breathlessly as they move. The leader, Thrimi, sings the verses and everyone joins the chorus. Her voice is clear and strong and her expression conveys the mood of the song. Her eyes are downcast and her expression reflective when she sings a sad song. She smiles and moves into a bouncy rhythm for a happy song.

The party is at Ap Tandi's house. He has held his *lochhoe* (annual ceremony for the family's well-being) that day and invited all his neighbours for the evening's festivity. The entire village is there. At dusk the men, women, and children sat in two rows in front of the house and were served the traditional evening meal of rice, pork and beef strips and Ap Tandi's legendary pumpkin stew, spiced with green chilli and hot pepper corn. Now the *ara* flows. Ap Tandi's wife, Aum Zam, is known to make a powerful brew from fermented wheat. She had loudly made her annual vow that nobody would leave her house until all her *palangs* (bamboo containers) were empty.

A few of the men and women, including Nado, are visibly tipsy as they sing and dance. Every song is greeted with shouts of appreciation, from the young and old alike. They shout requests for their favourite songs. As the men flock around Thrimi, gray haired Dophu - the wittiest man the village - shouts, "Thrimi, with her face like the full moon, has more admirers than the flies on Ap Tandi's dried meat." Everyone laughs. "Nado will get nowhere because he won't be able to stay on his feet for long." Everyone laughs again.

The older people sit close to the fire and children run around, playing their own games. A *palang* of *ara* tucked under his arm, Ap Tandi pours drinks for the dancers. "We will sing the *tashi lebey* (auspicious closing song) only at dawn so you can see your way home," he says, laughing. "We will not let Thrimi stop singing tonight."

Kuenley is fast asleep as his father carries him home a little before midnight. His school holidays are over and he leaves for Thimphu tomorrow. He lives there with his aunt who is married to a clerk in the finance ministry. Most of the villagers send their children to schools in Thimphu if they have relatives to live with because the village school is in Thinleygang, a two-hour walk. Children find it difficult to reach school in time for the morning prayers. And there are too many leeches when it rains.

***

New Times

Kuenley is 14-years old and home for the school holidays when the electricity lines to the village are completed. The village astrologer chooses an auspicious day for the inauguration ceremony. The astrologer and three lay monks start the prayers at dawn. The *dzongda*, the district's highest official, arrives at the auspicious hour of 9.00 am and turns on the transmission station below the village. "Our nights have turned into days because of the selfless service of our beloved King," he says. Thrimi leads a group of women in a selection of songs. Everyone has contributed ingredients for *suja-dresi* (butter tea and sweet rice) and nominated the village's best cook, Ap Dago, to make the *dresi*. The astrologer and the *dzongda* are served first and everyone else sits on the grass in two rows their cups and bowls placed in front of them for the *suja* and *dresi*.

Now the houses are brightly lit with naked bulbs at night. Children do their homework and women weave. The village is changing. The people are changing. Thrimi has married a 55-year old former government official who bought land from an old couple who have left the village to retire into a life of Buddhist practice. The couple sold their land because their two sons have both left home, one to join the civil service and one to become a monk.

Everyone calls Thrimi's husband *"dasho"* because he had been an official. He had resigned from the government and made money by becoming a trader. He has built a new house with the village's first zinc roof. It glistens in the sun, in stark contrast to the traditional wooden shingles that the others use. He also brought from Thimphu a large rice cooker, an electric pan to cook meat dishes, and a refrigerator. He has a special sitting room in his house, with a sofa set and two *choedroms* (tables), to entertain visiting officials.

Nado is a telephone line-man at the district telephone exchange. He left the village to look for a job. He is trained to look after the telephone line between the Thinleygang exchange and Lobesa. His parents still look after the herd, grazing them during the day and milking them in the morning and evening to produce butter and cheese. They sell the produce at the Thimphu market.

"No archery this year, huh?" Kuenley is sitting on the raised edge of a terrace. His childhood friend, Tenzing, is ploughing the field, his right hand on the plough handle, pushing the ploughshare into the ground to get a deep groove, his left hand guiding two oxen with a long wooden cane. Tenzing looks around at the rows of unploughed terraces. "It'll probably take me until *Losar* to finish these," he says.

Kuenley finds his friends changed every year. At 14 years he is in Class IX, a boy grappling with homework, obsessed with basketball. The 14-year olds in the village are men with adult responsibilities.

***

It is February. As they do every year, Kuenley and his mother go to Lobeysa village to make offerings at Chhimi Lhakhang, the 15th-century *lhakhang* (monastery) built by the popular saint, Drukpa Kuenley. Drukpa Kuenley strikes a chord in the Bhutanese people because of the outrageous antics he used to overcome evil and to expose the hypocrisy in society, including the religious hierarchy. His teachings are often expressed as graphic sexual exploits, symbolic of his "crazy wisdom".

The *lhakhang*, according to legend, is built on the spot where he subjugated the Dochu-la demoness who was terrorising the people in the valley. It sits on top of a dramatic hillock that resembles a giant breast. On most days a stream of pilgrims are seen on the bare grassy slope leading to the *lhakhang*. Many are pregnant and many carry babies to be named because Drukpa Kuenley is most revered for his blessings of fertility for which pilgrims come from all parts of the country. Kuenley's own parents had lost three babies before him and have no doubt that he survived because they made the pilgrimage to Chhimi Lhakhang when his mother was pregnant with him. So every year his mother packs rice, meat, fruit, and a bottle of alcohol to be offered to his "spiritual father".

They stop at the village shop in Lobesa valley to buy a packet of dalda (oil) and a roll of incense sticks. It is a warm afternoon, typical for Lobesa. Last year the government had introduced a second crop of paddy, in autumn, so the people had two harvests and doubled their income. But this year many families refused because it was too much work. They wanted the time for their winter festivals, archery matches, and the favourite winter pastime, basking in the sun.

A group of children are leaning on the open windowsill of the shop, gazing longingly at the variety of imported fizzy drinks in the store that they cannot afford. Some older village boys are gathered outside the shop to stare at the latest attraction in the village, a large glossy advertisement for a new soda drink.

The advertisement shows a fair-skinned dark-haired model lying on her side, her raised head resting on her left hand, propped up by the elbow. She is wearing a red bikini. Her slim body is sensuously poised so that the curve of her waist and hips resembles the "waist" of the bottle that she holds in her right hand. Her red bikini and the dark red liquid in the bottle contrast sharply against the blue backdrop of the billboard. But it is her bare arms, hips and thighs that are best accentuated in the picture.

"Is she made of plastic?" says one. They break into laughter. They are all in the late teens. Three of them are wearing grimy singlets and shorts that were once white. Two of them are wearing *ghos* with the tops taken off and sleeves wrapped around their waists.

"I don't know what she's made of but Drukpa Kuenley would know what to do with her," says another. They all laugh.

Kuenley is not amazed by the billboard because he has seen many of them in Thimphu. He has even watched television. His uncle's boss in Thimphu bought a television set when he went on a study tour to Bangkok. One day his uncle had sent him with some papers to the boss's house. The boss was not home so his wife had allowed Kuenley to wait in the sitting room where her son and daughter were watching a Hindi film.

Back in the village his friends ask him over and over again to repeat what he had seen on television. He can see the amazement in their eyes as he describes the handsome hero, in fine clothes, who fights dozens of bad guys and the heroine who literally glitters with make-up and fancy dresses that change even as she dances through fields and forests, over mountains and rivers, on trains, cars, and motorcycles.

***

Coming of age

"This is a precious load," says Kuenley's brother-in-law, Tshering. The cardboard box containing a 16-inch television set is strapped to his back. Kuenley follows him up the hill. He is 17 years old and has just finished school. Over the past year his family had sent his uncle bags of rice, rare orchids collected by Tshering, vegetables and fruits grown on the farm to be sold in Thimphu. His uncle had saved the earnings and bought the television set. Kuenley's parents had originally planned to buy a diesel-powered rice mill but his sister, 22-year old Yangzon, and her husband, Tshering, insisted on a television set. Two other families in the village already had television sets.

"I hope you are not going to carry the TV set around the village before you take it home," says Kuenley. Tshering has a tendency to

74

show off. He did that with a power thresher two years back. "Why not?" was Tshering's response. "Last year Ap Dophu carried a leg of beef around on his shoulder just to show us that he was going to eat meat."

For Yangzom, this is the big moment. She has cleared the *chhoesham* (altar) room and had the village carpenter make a special stand for the television set. It is placed in the corner opposite the altar, its glistening presence immediately commanding the room. She covers it with a piece of bright red polyester cloth to protect it from dust and soot. She places a vase of plastic flowers on top to prevent the cloth from slipping off. She is smiling.

***

The two girls stand on either side of the 21-inch television screen, facing the room. They are wearing short white T-shirts and tight blue jeans, with their midriffs exposed. One of them reaches out and switches on the DVD player on a shelf beneath the television set and on comes a Bollywood dance routine. The two girls gyrate with the line of women on the screen to the fast Hindi disco number, their hands up in the air, their hips rotating.

The audience, about 20 men and women and a dozen children of different ages, are mesmerised. Their eyes move from the screen to the two girls and back to the screen. Sitting in front, Aum Zam has her hand over her open mouth. Ap Dophu, standing a little unsteadily in the back of the room, is telling jokes but is inaudible because of the loud music. Kuenley, sitting on the floor near the open door to avoid the sweaty atmosphere in the room, gets an occasional whiff of scent from the girls. He just had his first taste of whiskey and feels grown up.

It is dasho's *lochhoe*. He has killed a fat pig and served slices of pork with fat that was four fingers thick. There is Special Courier whiskey and Dragon rum flowing. Dechen, dasho's 14-year old daughter from his former wife, has planned the modern entertainment for the villagers. Her best friend, Deki, who likes to be called "Diks", came for the *lochhoe* and to dance with her.

This is something the villagers have never seen before. The girls dance for an hour or so and then show some films they had brought from Thimphu. The guests are riveted to the screen. They do not understand the dialogue but are fascinated by the action. The older people go home because their sight is not so good. They prefer the outdoor dancing of their times.

Thrimi, now called Aum Thrimi because she is dasho's wife, serves drinks and food all evening. Her uncle, Dom Saymi, is not well these days. He lives alone.

Around midnight Kuenley goes home. Walking past the two girls, he fakes a little stagger to walk like the other men who have been drinking all evening.

***

It is around noon as Kuenley walks down the path to Dom Saymi's house. He leaves the next day and is a little sad because it might be a long time before he comes back to the village. His Class XII marks are good so it is likely that he will get a scholarship to India. He will opt for electrical or electronic engineering because he is one of the few students with very good mathematics results.

Dom Saymi is sitting on the bear-skin near the window, hunched over a half-finished rope. He looks much smaller than he was last year and his movements are feeble. He works with his face very close to the rope strands to see better.

Aum Thrimi is stirring broth on a small pot on the hearth. She is very busy these days. She runs the dasho's household and comes regularly to cook for her uncle.

"My mother says these herbs will be good for Dom Saymi. She got them from the lam when we went to Chhimi Lhakhang." He gives Aum Thrimi a clear plastic bag with a mixture of crushed brown leaves, twigs, and seeds.

"Oh good, I'll put it in his broth right now." She empties the herbs into the pot and stirs it for some time.

"So what kind of dances do the boys do these days?" she asks over her shoulder. "Modern girls dance just like the movie heroines." She takes the pot over to Dom Saymi and pours some broth into a cup on the floor in front of him. She sits next to him and rests her elbow on the windowsill, looking out.

"Men do the same dances, more or less." Kuenley visited a disco in Thimphu when his uncle gave him some money for passing his final exams. Everyone was writhing to loud music in the dim light. Many were smoking and nearly everyone was drunk. He did not quite understand why the senior students seemed so excited about going to the disco.

Aum Thrimi looks into the distance. "They are so pretty, the girls. They are so thin. They are so fair. They smell so nice."

She looks at Kuenley, a gangly five-foot nine-inch boy, standing with his hands in his pockets. She turns and looks out of the window again.

"Better study hard Kuenley. Otherwise you'll have to live in the village. You have to work all day in the sun. You have to walk everywhere with no shoes. You have to carry manure on your back and smell of cow dung. In the village you will quickly become ugly. We have no choice because we are already old and ugly."

Kuenley says nothing. He does not know what to say. Thrimi is 27 years old. She has not changed. But the world has.

In The Service Of The Nation

The dzong is silhouetted against the morning sky, its gilded pinnacle gleaming in the crisp air. The sun heightens the contrast between the red roof, the whitewashed walls, and multi-coloured artwork on the wooden door and window frames. This large monastic fortress, a 17th century architectural wonder, fits majestically into the contours of the high mountain ridge where it sits. Bhutanese craftsmen from different parts of the kingdom, each region boasting special skills, had come together to put together this massive edifice using only natural materials – mud, wood, and stone – without architectural drawings or powered tools and without a single nail.

All 20 districts of the kingdom are administered from the dzongs, a legacy of an era when Bhutan was governed, in a dual system, by spiritual and temporal rulers. They are still shared by the clergy and the civil administration. The official monk body performs ceremonies in the dzongs' altar rooms for the benefit of the kingdom, the world, and all sentient beings. Other parts of the dzongs house the civil administration, the offices of the local government and the district court. Built on strategic hilltops and ridges to ward off invaders in the 17th century, the dzongs symbolise the centrality of governance today.

***

Sherap learned all this as a student in Bhutan's first high school in Kanglung. This morning, however, he is oblivious to the mythological history and the physical grandeur of the dzong. Deep in thought he walks past the blue-clad police guards flanking the outer courtyard gate and along the cobbled path to the main entrance. The two large batwing wooden doors are kept open during working hours. The inner courtyard is aesthetically paved with rough flagstone that are set in the mud, their edges neatly hewn with hammer and chisel. Grass and weeds have pushed their way through the uneven cracks where they are joined, giving the courtyard a natural outdoor look.

He walks across the courtyard, sending a closely packed flock of pigeons, feeding on food crumbs lying on the flagstones, into flight, their fluttering wings sounding like a drum roll. He walks past several sleeping dogs to circumambulate the *utse* (central tower) and spins some prayer wheels, more out of habit than intent, before climbing up the steep flight of steps to the dasho's office. Outside the door he practices his bow, lowering his *kabney* (scarf) until the frills nearly touch the floor.

***

The dasho, who is responsible for the administration of the entire district, carries the poise of being a large man. About five-foot eleven inches, he is plump all round with his gray and black hair closely cropped and a small scattering of hair on his upper lip, not enough to warrant a shave. His skin is brown, the colour of a man who has grown up outdoors and he chews *doma* (betel nut) almost incessantly. He appears to lean back when he sits on his traditional high-back chair, a posture partly forced by a large stomach. He punctuates his speech with a disarming smile that makes his eyes crinkle and shows surprisingly white teeth although the lips and gums are stained red by betel nut.

He is in an expansive mood. "Oy Sherap, come, come… *zhu*," he says, magnanimously respectful to a junior official. He presses a switch that hangs on a red and white electrical cord from his desk. It rings a bell outside the door where his personal assistant sits behind a large Remington typewriter. "Bring us some tea," he tells the girl who walks in. "And bring me the letter to the health secretary when you finish typing it. I want Sherap to read it before I send it to Thimphu. He can make it flowery with his English Honours." He leans back on his swivel chair and laughs good naturedly, looking at Sherap.

Through the open windows behind the dasho Sherap can see the hill slope down to the floor of the valley. It is covered with terraced paddy fields, now bare in the winter. His mother would say it looks like his father's wrinkled brow. Through the window on his left he can see a part of the town, a row of 12 two-storey shop houses. The people call the town "baza", adapting the Hindi word "bazaar", after coming into contact with the hundreds of Indian officials, teachers, military men, and road workers who work in the kingdom.

***

Recently graduated from university in India on a government scholarship Sherap joined the civil service and was sent to the Mongar district office three months ago. It was a long-cherished dream come true. On July 10, 1978, he walked up the path towards this imposing dzong that represented officialdom. He was proudly conscious of the carefully-folded white *kabney* on his shoulder, symbolising his status as a government official.

"Don't you want to become a dasho and sit in the dzong all day?" his mother asked him several times a day as he grew up in Bumthang district. It was her reminder to wake him up on cold winter mornings for the hour-long walk to school and for him to do his homework by dim candlelight in the evenings. "Or do you want to work like this?" She would show him her palms, calloused by farm work.

He remembered his father going to the dzong one day, carrying a block of their best butter, wrapped in banana leaves, as a present for the dasho. "It is important for us to take nice gifts when we go to the dzong," his father told him. "Today, we get everything we need from the government."

***

"How was your tour?" asks the dasho, absent-mindedly scratching his right ear with a matchstick. He looks at a piece of white ear wax stuck on the match head when he pulls it out and blows it into a plastic waste basket near his feet.

"A couple suffering from leprosy did not want to come for treatment," says Sherap, his head bowed and voice lowered to show deference to the dasho.

"These people know nothing," says the dasho. "The government is spending so much money to cure them but they don't understand." His brows furrow and he shakes his head. "You see, they are so backward." His tone carries more sympathy than his words.

Sherap remains silent. He glances at a framed portrait of His Majesty the King on the wall behind the dasho. A white silk scarf is placed over the frame in reverence. All four walls of the office are painted sky blue, completely covered with hand-painted stylized white clouds. The wooden window frames are painted dark red. The wooden floor is polished and shines with the yellowish taint of artemesia leaves.

"You young people must teach them," says the dasho, the matchstick transferred to the left ear. "You have been given a good education by the government. Now it's time for you to serve the *tsawa sum* with loyalty and dedication."

Sherap has heard this numerous times throughout his school life. He is not quite clear about what *tsawa sum*, meaning the "three roots", stood for. Some interpret it as "king, government, and country" and some as "king, country, and people". These days witty young civil servants interpret it as "house, toyota, and apple orchard", taking a dig at senior civil servants who have acquired these symbols of physical comforts.

The dasho slurps loudly from a large blue china mug that his secretary has placed in front of him. He gestures to the white cup in front of Sherap. "Come, drink." Sherap picks up the cup and takes a sip of the thick sweet tea.

Sherap has been deeply pensive since the tour because he cannot get the couple, Tashi and Pem, out of his mind. Tashi is the first leper he has met. Pem is Tashi's wife. Sherap's visit to their house has had a vivid impact on him. His conversation with Pem has given him new insight into a world that he has not confronted yet. It has also left him feeling completely inadequate.

***

The dasho had sent him on a tour of 17 villages. His job was to explain an initiative started by His Majesty's sister, Ashi Kesang Wangmo. The government was setting up camps where people could be checked for leprosy and treated at an early stage. Those who were found infected would be kept in the camps for 30 days and treated. This was necessary because the new wonder drug for leprosy, Rifampicin, had to be taken for 30 days, one pill a day without a break. It could not be distributed because the villagers would forget to take them and this expensive drug would be wasted. To encourage leprosy patients to come for treatment the project was providing shelter and meals at the camp.

Sherap was excited about the tour. He liked the idea of walking through mountains and forests to the scattered villages. He saw visions of quiet treks through the pristine countryside, hot meals cooked over campfires, and peaceful nights under the clear skies. As an official he was entitled to a local guide in each village. The guide would carry his bedding and cook his meals. This was a luxurious way to learn about his country and people.

Besides, he was carrying good news. Here was the end of a terrible scourge. The dasho had already sent runners to the village headmen ordering them to survey the local communities for suspected leprosy infected people. Sherap's job was to record their names and villages so they could be called to the camps for diagnosis and treatment.

***

The first guide arrived four hours early. Sherap had planned to leave at about 9.00 am for the two-day walk to the first village, Kenkhar. His landlord knocked on his door at 5.00 am to inform him that the guide was waiting. Enthusiastic about his first official tour, Sherap got dressed and summoned the guide. The wiry man was about five feet tall, wearing a light *gho* with no shoes or socks. He did not speak Dzongkha, so Sherap decided that it was the right opportunity to learn the eastern dialect, Sharchhopkha. The man silently tied Sherap's bedroll and food bag together, strapped it on his back, and set off at a rapid pace.

Sherap had packed food from his landlord's store - rice, dried fish, radish, chillis, cooking oil, tea, and sugar. He planned to stop before midday and get the guide to cook a hot meal of rice, chilli, and butter tea by the river. This guide looked fit and could probably find some delicious wild orchids or mushrooms in the forests along the way.

The guide kept a relentless pace through the morning. Sherap struggled behind him, not wanting to complain. If this was the Bhutanese farmer's pace he would keep up with it. Several hours later, a tired, thirsty, and hungry Sherap shouted to the guide, who was walking ahead, to slow down. When Sherap caught up with him the guide offered him a cup of *ara* (fermented local brew) with some fried maize grain soaking in it. He offered the cup with both hands, bowing low and gesturing that Sherap should drink it. Relieved to get a break and a drink Sherap sat on a stone and drank it, chewing on the maize.

The *ara* made him light-headed and, by the time he ate the soaked maize, he was intoxicated. The guide set off suddenly, leaving Sherap no choice but to follow unsteadily. An hour later the guide poured him another cup of *ara* which he drank because they were not carrying water and there were no streams along the way. A little later, quite drunk, he drank some more *ara* and ate more maize grain. Sherap stumbled on through the day, trying to keep up with his guide who practically ran ahead without looking back.

They came to the edge of the village at about 10.00 pm that night. The guide stopped at the first house and asked the family to allow Sherap to stay the night. Sherap managed to open his bedroll and flop into bed. He was hungry and thirsty but too tired to wait for food. And he had a massive headache.

When he woke up the next morning he felt as if a yak had walked over him. After a 17-hour walk without eating or resting every muscle was aching and his head was throbbing. He also felt like an idiot, having let the guide take complete control of his journey. The guide must have taken advantage of him being a new official. He hauled himself up and, visibly angry, staggered out of the musty store room where he had slept to look for the guide.

The guide was nowhere in sight and his host, a maize farmer, explained in halting Dzongkha that he had returned home. The guide's wife, who was nine months pregnant, had started having labour pains the night before Sherap started his tour. He had no choice but to accompany Sherap because it was his duty to bring him to the first village of the tour. So he had pushed Sherap to do the two-day walk in a marathon stretch so he could rush home. "We have no hospitals and doctors," his host seemed to apologise for the guide. "Our children are as likely to die at birth as they are to survive. The mothers sometimes do not survive."

***

For the next two weeks Sherap walked from village to village. He ate delicious meals outdoors, rice and very spicy wild plants washed down with fresh whey that farmers gave him. Interestingly the cattle sometimes looked healthier than people and he was able to buy fresh milk and cheese even in remote villages. He was accompanied by different guides from one village to another. Some knew nothing apart from their farm work but some had interesting stories about their villages and people. When accompanied by talkative guides every mountain, river, waterfall, rock, cave, or footpath came to life through their stories, beliefs, and superstitions.

At night Sherap would be asked to stay at the best house in the village where he stopped, usually a very basic wooden structure. There was no electricity in this part of the country and the evenings were lit up with firewood that also warmed the houses. Community elders called on him, bringing bottles of *ara* as gifts. They would drink the *ara* they had brought and tell him their problems. They needed roads and drinking water and fertiliser. Then they would get drunk and start singing and dancing. The prettiest girls were encouraged to sing and dance close to the guest. "Our dashos from Thimphu must be happy," a drunk host explained one night.

Being the guest Sherap was always offered the best food and drink and the people themselves ate what was left. One night Sherap was invited to the house of a village elder for dinner because he had some dried pork, a rare delicacy. The adults drank *ara* and talked. Sherap could not eat because the children sat around him, staring hungrily at the piece of meat on his plate.

***

"So did you get any girls?" the dasho is in a talkative mood. "Be careful, huh, there is a lot of leprosy in this area." Sherap is flattered by the camaraderie in the dasho's voice but he lacks the confidence to share such banter. "And don't drink too much *ara* because you can get sick. Some families are believed to poison visitors with their alcohol."

Sherap has learnt that this is a widely held belief. Nearly every time he has walked passed a house he has been offered *ara*, even early in the morning. "Ara zhay-la, doo ma-la," they would say in the Sharchhop dialect, meaning "Have some *ara*, there is no poison." He himself concluded that it was superstition and the so-called poison may be just poor hygiene.

As for the women, Sherap was often attracted to girls in several villages but could not bring himself to take any initiative. The thought that some people had leprosy in the villages frightened him. The evening parties were fun but he could not launch himself into the public flirtation that was a norm and, from what he learnt, natural to many government officials who toured the villages.

***

Sherap had expected that people suffering from leprosy would be keen to attend the treatment camps. He thought they would be waiting to hear the details. He had prepared a patriotic speech in Sharchhop to explain that the government had drawn up this policy for the benefit of the people. After studying for so many years he had come to serve the people. He felt good about it.

But there were no lines of eager and grateful lepers waiting for him. He learned that, in the early stages, people did not know that they had contracted the disease. Those who did were needed in the fields and to fetch drinking water until they were too sick to work. He found that most people were reluctant to talk about the problem. Lepers were not blatantly ostracised but it seemed to Sherap that theirs was a silence shrouded in superstition, as if talking about it might make them more vulnerable to the disease.

Sherap also discovered that Bhutan was a land of short distances but long journeys. Sparsely scattered over the rugged terrain, houses were far from each other. A village might have only five houses but it would take more than a day to visit all of them. "It will be too much hardship for you to find lepers yourself," one village headman advised him. "And even if you do go to the people and strip them naked you cannot tell if they have leprosy until the late stages."

So Sherap was totally dependent on the names of people given to him by the village headmen and elders. His tour took on a pattern. He would be met by the local leaders when he arrived at a village. After Sherap had vehemently refused the bottles of *ara* that they offered as a greeting the representative would give him an incoherent oral report. There were no leprosy cases in some villages, some reported suspected cases, and some reported two or three people who were known to have leprosy. The headman had heard all this from villagers who had heard it from other villagers. That was their survey.

***

One night Sherap slept in a temple above a village. Soon after dinner his guide and the temple caretaker disappeared, supposedly to organise his meeting the next day but obviously to look for *ara* in the village. Sherap was alone, but not lonely. As he lay on the uncovered deck of the temple the only light in the dark world around him came from the stars in the clear sky. They looked like millions of butter lamps sitting on a vast altar. The only sound came from the surrounding forest, the occasional howl of a wolf, the whooping of an owl and, once, the roar of a larger animal.

Under that magic sky Sherap suddenly felt a surge of guilt. He was nearly at the end of the tour and all he had was a list of suspected leprosy cases gathered by word of mouth. The village headmen assured him that this was how all official tours were conducted but that did not comfort him. He had not even seen a single leper himself. He had stayed in the best houses, ate the best food, drank *ara*, but had done nothing that was remotely beneficial to the people.

That was why Sherap met Tashi and his wife, Pem. On the 11th day of the tour he arrived at their village after a three-hour climb up a narrow path that zig-zagged almost vertically for 3,000 feet from the floor of the valley. He had sent his guide ahead to inform the headman that he did not want just a list of people. He wanted to talk to a leper himself.

***

Tashi and Pem's hut stood on the edge of the village. The walls and roof made of locally woven cane mat plastered with mud to make it wind proof. It looked like a temporary structure. A thin wisp of blue smoke wafted through one corner of the roof.

Once inside, Sherap closed his eyes and opened them again to get accustomed to the dim light. A woman, who he guessed was Pem, was sitting near a small square opening in the wall that served as a window. Her coarse and faded *kira* was worn high and her strong brown calves bulged a little as she sat, cross-legged, on the roughly hewn planks that covered half the room. The other half of the floor was mud. Her hair was closely cropped and arms bare.

She looked like she was in her 50s but that meant nothing. After about 30 years out in the fields, working from dawn to dusk almost throughout the year, her skin had taken on the rough texture that was a natural effect of severe wear and tear.

She quickly stood up when he entered and shyly gestured to him to sit, bowing low: "Zhu-la". She poured a cup of what he guessed was *ara* from an old bamboo flask beside her, brought it to him and placed it on the floor in front of him.

Sherap remained standing.

"I am ashamed that I have nothing else to offer you," she said. "I don't dare offer you anything in my dirty house. Please don't mind." She walked back to the corner of the room where the man lay, covered by a blanket. She sat near him, a little protectively it appeared to Sherap.

The man did not look at him. He had no eyebrows and the dull eyes in the gaunt face stared at the ceiling. As the woman spoke to Sherap he pulled the blanket up to his neck, using the two stubs that were left of his hands after his fingers had fallen off. Sherap had learnt enough about leprosy to know that he had no toes.

Sherap's throat was dry. He fought back an intuitive mixture of repulsion and sympathy. His guide had told him that he would not get infected by being in the same room with a leper. But the guide had probably heard this from a villager who had heard it from another villager.

***

The conversation is stuck in Sherap's mind, in graphic detail. It is a vivid scene that keeps re-playing in his head like a tape recorder.

"I have good news," Sherap says, the words sounding completely futile. "We will establish a leprosy camp in Lhuntse and treat your husband. You have to stay just one month."

"It's too late," she answers, looking at her husband.

"It's not too late for you. Even if you have caught it the new medicine can stop it."

"What for?"

He has no immediate answer.

"He is a good man," she adds, somewhat defensively. "He used to plough two *langdos* a day. He could carry 30 *dres* of wheat to the market. He carried me for five days to the hospital when I was sick."

"Don't you have a family?"

"He's my family."

"Children?"

"We have a son. He went to look for a job as a truck driver. We don't know where he is."

Sherap understands that. Many young men in eastern Bhutan want to become truck drivers. They make money carrying people and goods over the harsh mountain roads and that gives them status. People line the roads asking truck drivers for rides and to help transport their farm produce to the market. Truck drivers have many girlfriends because it is a glamorous job.

"But what will you do here, if you are alone?" Tashi shows no sign of having heard anything.

"This is my home."

Sherap looks around the small hut. In one corner, behind the man's head, is a rectangular cane basket with a cover. It must hold their personal belongings. In another corner, behind Sherap, is a small hearth. There are three small soot-blackened aluminum cooking pots hanging above it. The bamboo water container, five stems tied together, stands beside the hearth. A rope is stretched along the ceiling above the man with a few items of clothing hanging from it.

***

Sherap thinks about his own room. He had shared bedrooms with his brother and two sisters until he went to high school where he had slept in a dormitory with 45 other boys, on two long rows of beds. This is the first time that he has lived alone and he does not think about it as "home". He rents the room from a businessman who runs a grocery store downstairs, selling all the basic necessities that farmers around the valley need. These range from clothing and blankets to food grain like rice, sugar, and salt imported from India and vital essentials like matchboxes, torch batteries, and aluminum cooking utensils. One wall is lined with shelves carrying cheap whiskey, rum, and beer.

He has pasted old newspapers on all four walls of his room to keep the wind from coming in through the cracks between the wood panels as much as to stop the owner's curious rural relatives who visit regularly from peeping into the room. The room is Sherap's new identity, containing all his possessions. Two cotton mattresses are laid on top of each other, on the plain wooden bed. The sheets and pillowcases, with brightly coloured patterns on them, are imported from India, like the three checked woollen blankets that he uses.

From two wooden pegs high on the wall hang the two *ghos* he had bought from the landlord's shop, one plain gray and the other a traditional blue-and-red checked mathra. When he returns from office he hangs his *kabney* on a long nail near the *ghos*. Two pairs of leather calf-length boots, one black and one brown, and a pair of white canvas shoes are lined against the wall below the *ghos*.

Two steel trunks sit under the bed, containing a mixture of clothes, including a fancy raw silk *gho* that his uncle had given him.

∗∗∗

"I hope you will remember the problems that you saw in our remote villages," says the dasho. "Otherwise, when you sit in a ministry in Thimphu, you will not know what the people need."

They are drinking their second cups of tea. The dasho is satisfied with the neatly typed list of suspected lepers. They will be called after the camps are set up. The village headmen and elders will be summoned for the opening ceremony. He will give a speech. He asks Sherap to draft a respectful letter to Ashi Kesang Wangmo to come and open the camp.

***

Back in his room that evening Sherap thinks about Tashi and Pem. He wonders how many more people there are in the remote villages, like Tashi and Pem, resigned to their fates. He remembers Pem's innocent question. What does she have to live for by staying alive after her husband dies? This stoic woman prefers to die with her husband because of what they once shared.

Sherap has written essays about serving the *tsawa sum* throughout his school life. He has studied English, Science, and Mathematics. He has a university degree. But he has no answer for Pem. People like her need something that people like him cannot give. At the same time she seems at peace with her fate while he is completely disturbed by his first official tour.

Sherap gets up from the bed where he is sitting and walks over to his desk. He picks up the bottle of *ara* on the desk and pours some into an enamel cup and gulps it down. His throat smarts and his eyes water as he swallows the powerful liquid.

Serving the people is a more complex task than he had realised.

Karma

Karma

Karma came to our house two days before we left for Japan. "Can you drop me at the taxi stand?" he said. "I'm off to Paro to drink myself to death." He shook the blue and white tennis bag slung over his right shoulder until we heard the clink of bottles.

I cannot remember what we talked about as I drove him through the town. He was, as usual, a little dishevelled, his breath smelling of the shot of Black Mountain whiskey that was his cure for a hangover. "Hey, take it easy," my wife called out as he climbed out of the car. "See you in three weeks."

We never saw him again. Eight days later I woke with a start at

3.00 am, in a hotel room in Tokyo, knowing that he had died. I was touched that he had thought it worthwhile to say goodbye. We had been friends for 34 years.

***

Death is about life. It is death that brings the living together. This powerful symbol of "impermanence" is one of the most important teachings in Buddhism. When people discuss death they find themselves talking about the living. Even in Gyeltshen's bar.

Gyeltshen's Bar was the source of Karma's Black Mountain whiskey. On winter evenings he would buy a shot of whiskey, fill the rest of the glass with hot water and gulp it down. Then he would have another, and another, as Gyeltshen's regular customers came in to "bullshit each other", a Thimphu euphemism for idle chatter. He was not comfortable in the more up-market "restaurant-cum-bars" of the capital city where the urban elite – government officials, big time contractors, tour operators, foreign volunteers – exchanged political gossip over Bhutan Mist whiskey, Golden Eagle, and Dragon rum.

***

"He deserved what he got," says 60-year old Gyeltshen, owner of Gyeltshen's Bar, gruffly. "The *tsagay* (idiot) didn't know what was good for him. He would never listen to anyone. I'm not surprised." The old man wipes a tear with his dirty sleeve.

"Do you know that Karma was probably the first Bhutanese marijuana addict?" a sozzled civil servant asks his buddies. "We used to call him 'the joint director'. On a sunny day he would always be among the wild cannabis plants rubbing the oil onto his hands. Those days Bhutanese people who had not travelled outside the country didn't know that it could be smoked so the village girls collecting the plant to feed their pigs didn't know what the hell he was up to."

"Maybe that's why the bugger read books I could never understand," says a tour guide. "He kept a translation of Milarepa's poems under his pillow".

**

I, Karma's classmate for 10 years, knew all about that. He had always been more intellectually mature than his peers. In our boarding school in northern India Karma was reading Albert Camus and Joseph Conrad when his classmates read Mills and Boons romance novels that were dumped in missionary-run schools in the third world by charity organisations in the west. For essays he wrote satires that teachers did not understand and derided in class. In junior school I remember him smuggling Mad magazines into the dormitory and reading them under his blanket by torchlight because teachers considered them decadent reading.

***

"He was very gullible and fell into all sorts of traps," says another regular at Gyeltshen's Bar, a driver of the World Food Programme office where Karma found a job. "A loose woman in eastern Bhutan once knocked him out with *ara* and dragged him under her blankets. The next morning she demanded the load of bulgar wheat meant for the entire village and he could shut her up only by giving her his month's salary. I don't think he even touched her. He himself didn't have a clue."

"That's nothing compared with what happens here in Thimphu," says a health technician on a barstool. "I refused to go to the Philippines for a training programme because all my colleagues have been eyeing my wife. It's very Bhutanese, you know. We thought our rural vasectomy programme was a failure when the women kept getting pregnant. We eventually found that they were sleeping with men other than their husbands."

***

I met Karma in the Indian town of Kalimpong in 1965, at Bhutan House, an office which coordinated the funds for Bhutanese students sent to English-medium boarding schools by the government. We were both seven years old when I first saw him, astride a wooden stick that was meant to be a horse and, on his head, a clear plastic bag that was supposed to be a helmet. As scholarship students we were sent by the education office to an Indian cloth store where all Bhutanese students were fitted with trousers, shirts, and socks because such "western" clothing was not available in Bhutan.

He had already spent a year in school and, as a new student entering the same boarding school five days' journey from home, I was glad to have a friend. I soon discovered that Karma was the butt of many jokes in the dormitory. He had not learned to control his bowels at night and the other kids in the dormitory laughed every time the "housemother" spanked him for dirtying his pyjamas or when he cried in his sleep which he did quite often.

**

"Karma's mother died giving birth to him," his uncle in eastern Bhutan told me years later. "When he was three his father shot himself for reasons that the boy will never know. After he turned seven he had an uncle who took him to boarding school every year but Karma later found out that the uncle was doing it only because he was after the family land in Paro. This uncle was later found murdered on the smugglers' trail near the Tibet border."

Every winter the Bhutanese students all travelled home together from school on buses organised by the Bhutanese government. Karma would disappear with a different relative every year and return to school somehow seeming more exposed to the world than the rest of us.

In his teens he was doing what most teenagers wanted to do but didn't dare. I was made school captain in 1975, a position that was perhaps allocated too much power in the old British tradition, and was once asked to deal with a "disciplinary situation" because a senior boy was found smoking a cigarette in the dorm. It was an awkward moment for both of us when the boy brought to the prefects' room the next day was my childhood friend, Karma. The embarrassment, for both of us, was more painful than any disciplinary action I could think of.

***

"One thing that Karma did; he always kept his word," another regular at Gyeltshen's Bar, Sonam, remembers. "If you invited him for dinner and he said 'yes' he would always turn up no matter how drunk he was. Most Bhutanese never do, and they never call to say that they can't come."

"He was particular about time," says Yuhani, Karma's school friend. "He was once supposed to take his older brother on the two-day journey to Samtse for an important meeting. His brother was not ready at 7.00 am as they had agreed so he left him behind."

***

Bhutanese youth who spoke English in the 1970s, the dozen or so students from boarding schools who went to Thimphu for the winter holidays, would hang out with the most elite section of society. The Swiss Bakery, the only modern cafeteria in the country, was the place to be. As students we would wait outside the bakery until a generous person like the king's cousin, Dasho Benji Dorji, came by and invited everyone in for coffee, beer, and meat patties.

With Bhutanese society in rapid transition we developed a culture of camaraderie, born out of common interests nurtured by our modern education. We were all children of a subsistence farming society that was completely cut off from the rest of the world. We were, by fortune more than design, headed for good jobs in a new government, endowed with responsibilities beyond our ages. We were part of a change that we did not quite comprehend.

Confused by Christian missionaries in boarding schools, some of whom ranted against our Buddhist upbringing, and unconvinced by our own domestic rituals that we did not understand, we veered between an intuitive protectiveness of our traditions and the objectivity of the Judeo Christian values that we had picked up.

We started losing touch with our roots, and with our values, as the paddy fields of Thimphu village were swallowed up by the concrete structures of Thimphu city. The plush Swiss Bakery became a venue for new customs like disco dances and birthday parties. Trendy globalised parents in the 1980s and '90s were encouraging children to consume large volumes of sweet pastries and started bestowing on them plastic Barbie and Power Ranger dolls.

***

Karma preferred the crude jokes of Gyeltshen's Bar to the exchange of jet-set experiences in the Swiss Bakery. As a WFP employee he chose to travel around rural Bhutan delivering grain and other food supplies to village communities and schools. He liked the long journeys and difficult treks to remote places.

When our son turned one year we had not thought of inviting Karma to his birthday party. He would have looked odd among balloons and cakes and the plastic toys. Weeks later he heard that our son had turned one and came to the house with a small furry puppy of a pure Tibetan Mastiff for our son. This yak dog soon grew into a big shaggy member of the family and, in the years that he lived with us, he once fought off a leopard.

***

As a young boy Karma had the red cheeks like many Bhutanese children whose blood vessels were dilated by the cold mountain air and chilling winds. His fair skin and crop of unusually curly hair accentuated it enough to make adults pinch his cheeks, throwing him into great consternation. At the nickname, "Rosy", used by some teachers and older girls, his entire face would turn red, his body would concoct, and his slight stutter would become a severe one.

In the 1960s and '70s young Bhutanese students were returning home from boarding schools dressed in fashionable western clothing but shed them for the traditional *gho* and *kira* when they began working. Karma managed to maintain his untidy look with the clothes hanging on his thin, five-foot seven-inch frame. He did not like the bright machine-made textiles that became fashionable. He wore the old hand spun woollen clothes that were usually badly tailored because they were too thick for sewing machines.

Karma's apartment was a permanent open house. Friends dropped in at odd times in various stages of intoxication. A pot of tea on the stove would be emptied and refilled through the day. Local *ara* brewers stopped by to leave bottles of *ara*. They would come in the first of every month, pay-day, to collect.

***

"I think he should never have married."

That is the pragmatic wisdom in Gyeltshen's Bar. "These days you have to buy a refrigerator, a TV set, video player, car, and other things to keep a wife," says a schoolteacher. "It is not enough to be a good man or even a good husband."

"Karma was not an easy man to live with anyway," says Choden, Gyeltshen's 14-year old daughter who speaks with the authority of a teenager who has seen countless relations start and end at the bar. "His lifestyle would have been a nightmare for any woman."

"When she left him he was hurt more than he knew," says Thuji. "He started drinking heavily right from the morning. He stopped going to work. I stayed with him for a week. He seemed lost. I think he had become too dependent on her."

"Men," says Choden.

***

Karma never stopped drinking since he left school. It took its toll.

"I am very concerned about your behaviour," his boss told him one day.

"I am good at my job," said Karma.

"I have been informed that your drinking habit is affecting your work," his boss said.

"I drink in my own time," said Karma.

"I am also informed that you use drugs," his boss said.

"Marijuana is not a drug," said Karma.

Nobody knew whether the office fired him or whether Karma quit.

It didn't matter.

***

In Doti village of Paro the neighbours heard that Sangay's brother, Karma, had died. They all left their fields and went over to her house. The village elders requested the monks from the monastery above the village to come and perform the last rites. They consulted the astrologers who analysed the lunar forces and advised them to perform the cremation after three days.

Some men went off into the forest to collect wood for the cremation. Others prepared the pyre. Two young men, who were born under the animal signs that were auspicious for Karma, who was born in the year of the rooster, washed the body and wrapped it in one of his own *ghos*. The women took over the household chores. They prepared tea and food, first for the seven monks performing the ceremonies and then for the men and women of the village who came to console Sangay.

The response of the farmers was spontaneous. It was a tradition drawn from the interdependence among people within a community who relied on each other in times of trouble. Sangay's neighbours stayed with her until the cremation was over and the ash was collected. Then they all went home to their busy farm routines.

They had never met Sangay's brother. But they knew he was a good man. He had sent her money to pay for electrical fittings when the local electricity transmitter was installed in the village. He had helped her pay for a new roof three years ago. He sent her money every year for her annual ceremony. Last year he bought her two oxen for her farm.

"He didn't suffer," Sangay said. "On the morning that he died, he

asked us to move him near the window so he could look outside."
Sangay's family could not read the English words that Karma had
scrawled on a cabinet at his bed head:

Violets are blue
Roses are red
My life is mine
Until I am dead

***

"I would have gone to the cremation," says Tashi, pouring a shot of
Black Mountain into his empty glass at Gyeltshen's Bar. "But I had
this important meeting that day."

"I'm glad Karma was cremated in Paro," says Thuji. "In Thimphu
a cremation is politics. People attend if they want to be seen. It
has become important to have a long convoy of cars in the funeral
procession, to provide an elaborate buffet meal, to host a large
congregation of monks."

"Nobody told me the cremation was on Tuesday," says Yangchen,
"I would have been there."

"Unfortunately I was in Phuentsholing, on tour" says Tshering.

"What? Karma's dead?" asks Phuntsho, who walks into the bar.

"You people," says Choden.

HARSH WINDS

The mule slips on the wet ice and slides down the steep track. The man springs forward and grabs it by the muzzle. They both strain against the slope, breaking the skid on the edge of the sheer precipice. The mule is on its belly, its forelegs dangling over the cliff. Braced precariously, inches from edge, the man strains to hold the animal on the narrow track. Within seconds the man's teenage son, who was walking ahead of them, runs back and deftly unloads the mule, handing over the heavy packs to the woman who is holding the animal by its tail. Together they haul the mule back on to the path.

Far below them the mist swirls over the jagged rocks that line the bottom of the deep gorge.

A few metres behind, a 73 year-old woman sits on the icy path, inching forward on her buttocks, using both her hands and feet to maintain her balance. She watches calmly as her son, daughter-in-law, and grandson save the family mule and stock of rice for the summer.

Another few metres behind her the sweat beads on my forehead quickly freeze in the mountain air. I avoid looking over the edge as I follow the family, scanning the path intently for the best footholds.

**

Hours later, along with several other families spread along the path, we reach a swift stream at the base of the mountain. Without a thought the men, women, children hitch up their ghos and kiras to the waist and wade across, oblivious of the water which is close to zero degrees centigrade. Young men pass lewd remarks at the women who are forced to expose their upper thighs to avoid getting their *kiras* wet. The women shoot back quick witty remarks.

The path climbs again, up the next ridge. By evening, families are camped in caves and under leafy trees over the steep mountainside. The terrain is inhospitable, with no flat land to set up campsites.

The men care for the horses and tie them to tree trunks for the night while the women set up make-shift hearths to prepare hot meals of rice and chilli. By dark, after a few bottles of *ara* and sinchang men, women, and youth are exchanging raunchy stories.

***

It is early April, 1997, and the Layaps are heading home. Of the 60,000 semi nomadic population spread across the kingdom's northern region about 800 live in Laya, grazing about 2,000 yaks over the north-western grasslands of Bhutan's largest and most sparsely populated district, Gasa.

In the winter months the nomads move to the warmer valleys of Bhutan to trade. Starting in late October, when nature gives them a respite between the rain and the snow, the men move south with their mules. They carry butter, cheese, high altitude incense plants from the wilderness and sometimes dried fish, shoes, and brick tea that they trade across the Tibet border. Closer to the market they slaughter yaks. Yak meat and dairy products are highly sought after throughout Bhutan and the Layaps trade them for rice, oil, salt, sugar, chilli, and clothing. By May they will start moving the yaks up into the high mountains, from camp to camp, until the grasslands give way to the snow-covered peaks.

***

This year I join the Layaps on their journey home from Punakha valley, the nearest town and their main trade stop. The four-day walk is stretched over two weeks as they relay the year's food supply on mules and then yaks. The path slopes gently upwards along the Mochu river for a day and a half and then rises steeply to the 9,405 feet crest where the 17th century Gasa Dzong sits.

On the second day of the journey we catch our first glance of the dzong. As we walk around a bend it suddenly appears in the distance, a commanding white structure perched high on the northern ridges that provide a deep blue background. The people take off their caps in reverence and murmur prayers. I take my hat off, awestruck by the spectacle of this historic edifice. The dzong looks close enough to touch but is still half a day's climb.

Gasa is a popular stop. As they reach the base of the mountain men, women, and mules plunge into half a dozen hot springs by the river. Most herders camp at the hot springs, eating rice and chillis, drinking heated *ara*, to soak away a year's fatigue from their bones. The sense of tranquillity is best conveyed by the mules which stand ecstatically still in a large hot pool that is reserved for animals.

As a quiet dark descends on the valley and the mood gets lighter with *ara*, young men and women are outrageously open as they flirt in the pools. The men reach out to grab the women. The women playfully push them away and taunt them. The older people look on with patient understanding.

***

After Gasa the trail spirals through the clouds to one of the most spectacular regions in the kingdom. I hear the pounding of my heart in my head as the path climbs up steeply through the mixed conifer forests above Gasa dzong, to the Barila pass, over 12,000 feet. The entire mountainside is covered with maple, rhododendron, and groves of birch, juniper, and mountain canes. The wild flowers change shades through the year, like a massive carpet being changed, their patterns indicating spring, summer, and fall.

"This is one of the mildest seasons that I can remember," a village headman, Ap Tshering, tells me. "We can see the path. Sometimes the path lies under waist-deep snow and families are often stuck in blizzards. Last year three young men fell over the cliff where the mule skidded. Two of them carried back their dead friend." It is not unusual for men and pack mules to go over the edge and, sometimes, an entire mule caravan can plunge into the ravines.

Climbing up to the rugged Kohilapcha pass, the path crosses the tree-line and goes through the vast Alpine grasslands that undulate towards the great northern glaciers. All along the way crystal waterfalls spray the cliffs and run down the mountainside as rapid streams. Their sources, the turquoise glacial lakes that sit above the villages, are held in awe and reverence by the people.

This is the world where the snow leopards roam, where the blue sheep, sambar and musk deer graze in solitude. Lower down, the takin, the Himalayan black bear, numerous deer and wild dogs share the habitat. The winged inhabitants of the region include the raven, wild pheasants, snow pigeons, the red billed chough, the alpine swift, the snow partridge and the black-necked crane.

Spreading upwards from 12,000 feet above sea level, Laya sits on the lap of the 23,430-foot Masagang, one of Bhutan's 20 virgin peaks that are above 20,000 feet. I climb on to the edge of a sheer cliff directly opposite Masagang. I nearly lose my balance in a sudden and harsh gust of wind. I scramble down, breathless and frightened.

***

The Layaps call their home *baeyul*, the hidden land, with good reason. The cluster of villages is completely hidden by ridges and suddenly explodes into view when the traveller reaches the first houses. The people believe that they are protected by the aura of an ancient gate leading to the main village. "When we were attacked by Tibetans our guardian deities turned all these stones and trees into soldiers who fought them off," says Ap Tshering, pointing to the boulders and growth of spruce, fir, and rhododendron trees with an undergrowth of dwarf junipers.

Legend and history merge as I listen to Laya's elders. This was the place where Zhabdrung Ngawang Namgyal entered Bhutan in 1616 to eventually build the Bhutanese polity. In a journey which resounds with conquests of human and supernatural dimensions, the Zhabdrung crossed the chain of mighty Himalayan ridges and entered Laya. The Layaps pay homage to the footprints of the Zhabdrung and his horse, now enclosed in a *chhorten* in a small meadow called Tajekha below the villages.

***

The Layaps draw their identity from their rugged backdrop. The pristine mountain ranges have not succumbed to changes over the centuries. Neither have its people.

The men wear *ghos* similar to other Bhutanese men but the women wear distinct *kiras*, woven from yak hair, and cane hats. Physically, the people are as weather-beaten as the Alpine rangelands and can be as untamed and unpredictable. That is why the frustrations of district authorities who find that the Layap cannot be bound to deadlines and official responsibilities. "When you call them to the office they always say 'yes' but never turn up," explains an official of Gasa dzongkhag. "Call a Layap family to contribute labour for a government project and it is likely that a grandmother, who is not needed at home, will turn up."

Survival has sharpened the wiles of the Layap. It is a nightmare for dzongkhag officials to pin a Layap herder down on the number of yaks in his herd to tax them. They know that no civil servant will go and count hundreds of yaks spread over the ranges.

They are called *bjops* by other Bhutanese, a term that carries derogatory connotations. "The Layaps smell," says a civil servant. "You cannot depend on the Layaps," says a district official. "The Layaps are backward," says a Punakha farmer. "The Layaps are alcoholics," says a trader.

Sadly these come from sections of society that claim to be more developed. It takes just a few days among the Layaps in their homeland to see in them a raw honesty that is stripped of artificiality. "These people see you for what you are, with no pre-conceived notion," says Dr. Pema Jamtsho, who has lived there for four years. "In Thimphu, people look at you to see what they can get out of you."

The Layaps are also as open as their environment, normally free of social inhibitions. Men and women are open and relaxed on issues like the boundaries of sexual behaviour. This, in fact, is often exploited by occasional visitors like tourist guides, military patrolmen and civil servants who flirt with Laya women who are known for their beauty.

Inside the rough Layap exterior is a tenderness which is invisible to the casual observer. Every Layap identifies with a 46-year old horse owner who risked his life last year to scale an icy cliff to his horse which had fallen. The man was oblivious to the bitter cold as he sat with his dying horse for two days, feeding the animal water from his cupped palm, the water mixed with his tears.

The Layaps are most tender in their feelings for the yak which is the mainstay of their semi nomadic existence. They officially own about 2,000 of Bhutan's 35,000 yak population, both believed to be reduced figures. This beast of burden, weighing 300 to 400 kilogrammes, is a source of food, shelter, draught power, transportation and a part of the Layap identity.

"The yak is a parent," a 70-year old woman told me. "It is the source of our lives." Government livestock specialists explain that there is unwanted pressure on the pastureland because the nomads refuse to cull the old animals. Most Layaps claim that, apart from what is absolutely necessary for their annual trade, they will not kill the yak. But yaks, sometimes owned by wealthier people who live in the lower regions, are known to "fall over the cliff" regularly when the herders need meat.

∗∗∗

The carefree lifestyle comes with serious alcohol consumption. Nearly every man drinks heavily, sometimes losing time, effort, and hard earned money in drunken stupors. The people convert much of their food grain into alcohol. Sixty-three year old Ap Sangay is a typical example of the Layap man: "I have lived a hard life," he says with a proud smile. "Now I have two important goals in life. I brew *singchhang* (local wine) during the day and I drink it at night."

In this patriachal society where girls are married early and move to the husband's home, polyandry is on the decline. With clear cut gender roles the woman bears a serious domestic responsibility, looking after the yak herds, digging the fields, weaving the traditional clothing and generally keeping the home and family together. The men are responsible for trade and the transportation of goods, their own and for the government.

They share a strong community spirit and are fiercely protective of the image of their community. Internal squabbles are normally settled within the community and even a child will not divulge the name of a Layap who is guilty of some wrongdoing.

They are proud of their self-sufficiency in the basic necessities of life despite the day-to-day physical difficulties. Yak products account for 49 percent of the Layap's earning while 32 percent comes from trade, 15 percent from animal transport, and four percent from tourism, the last benefiting only five or six horse owners who are in contract with tour operators in Thimphu. "The herders are rich," says a district official. "Their storeroom walls are lined with rice bags, they have more than people in other villages around the country.

***

There is a strong spiritual element in the cohesion of the Layap community. The men pay obeisance to their Pho-Lha, the local guardian. Every archery match, every business trip, every journey, every development project starts with a prayer at the Pho-Lha's sacred shrine, a small *chhorten* above the village.

Like the broader Bhutanese society the advice of the village astrologer is sought on most activities and the local medium is usually consulted during illnesses. It is a legacy of the Zhabdrung that the Layaps celebrate the Bumkor festival to plant barley and the Aulay festival during harvest.

Superstition is strong and is, in fact, one of the protective forces of the Layap identity. "We believe that if the women stop wearing their distinctive *kira* we will disappear," says Ap Tshering's wife. Superstition, etiquette, and other aspects of the local traditions are often inseparable.

***

It is largely the exposure on their trading trips that have given the Layaps a view of a rapidly changing world outside their mountain abode. A handful venture to the capital, Thimphu. They are increasingly aware, with more than a little dismay, of the widening gap between their mountain life and the rapidly growing towns in lower valleys.

The urge to reach out and pluck the fruits of progress which their fellow citizens are enjoying is beginning to gnaw at the roots of the Layap culture. Thirty-year old Dodo wants to build a house like the one he saw in Punakha. His wife believes a road will solve all Layas problems. A young girl envies the Punakha schoolgirls in their modern *kiras*. An eight-year old boy rolls his father's hat around the campfire, his mind on the plastic toy cars he has seen in Punakha.

Two women who were selected to visit Thimphu as part of a cultural entertainment team returned embarrassed about their traditional *kiras* because they were clumsy compared with the soft nylon *kiras* of the Thimphu women. When told by a Thimphu official that the beautiful and unique Laya *kira* should be preserved one retorted: "So you can send tourists to take photographs of us?"

***

It is an enlightened policy that the government of Bhutan has sensitively pursued in the mountains of Laya. The goal is to improve the lives of the people without upsetting the delicate balance in their distinct cultural identity, the pristine natural ranges, and the rich wildlife.

Tuned to the migratory pattern of the people, the priorities reflect an emphasis on improving the yak herds and fodder, improving crop yields, and on building a motor road. A development goal for 2000, for example, was to raise the payment for porters and horses to increase the income of the people by about 80 percent.

Development is identified as the establishment of a basic health unit, a veterinary centre, and a school. Last year just two women died in childbirth and animal health has been greatly increased, along with their numbers. The Layaps, however, place their long-term hopes on about 100 children who are enrolled in a local primary school.

They are painfully aware of the image of backwardness they portray to other sections of Bhutan's population. A 56 year-old herder summed up the sentiments of all Layaps: "Last month, when we went to Thimphu, my son read the number on the bus ticket and showed me where to sit," he said, glowing with pride. "I did not have to face the shame of sitting in the wrong seat and other people laughing at me."

"Change? It is already here," says Ap Sangay, well into his fourth bottle of *singchhang*. "When I was a young man, I carried 40 *dre* of rice every year from Punakha on my back. It took me eight days. Now these boys have a motor road to Damji, cutting the journey in half. What more do they want?"

***

Ten days later, I steer my Toyota pick-up into Thimphu, a relatively massive city of 50,000. Laya and Thimphu represent the tensions of the contrast between Bhutan and the world. Laya confronts an issue which Bhutan, as a nation, has been grappling with for the past four and a half decades. How do we balance the harmony with our natural environment, how do we preserve the deep pride in our unique cultural identity against forces of change?

"We Layaps have our good points and bad points," explains one village elder. "But, in the end, our biggest pride is our land and ourselves. Yes we go out to trade, buy supplies, to drink, to flirt. We complain about our hardships, the heavy workload, the difficult road. We are embarrassed about our backwardness. But we would never want to be anything but a Layap."

But I cannot help a tingling of fear. Change is inevitable. Will the experience be more harsh than the bitter winds which blow over the mountains ?

An Episode

Bhutan has a rich tradition of stories, a mix of folklore and mythology, much of it drawn from ancient Buddhist scriptures. Among the most popular of the fireside stories are the outrageous antics of Lam Drukpa Kuenley. This episode is written from the writer's memory of his father's fireside tales.

The *kongyer* (caretaker monk), a chubby red-robed figure balancing a wooden tray of *tormas* (butter sculpture religious offerings) in one hand and an altar dust cloth in the other, walks to the door of the temple and sees a man standing outside the outer door of the alcove of the *lhakhang*. The visitor is an unwashed man dressed in a black *gho* that hangs untidily on his body. He is a little unsteady as he opens the door and steps in. He is wearing a pair of old leather shoes with no socks.

The *kongyer* is wearing a white bandana over his mouth, tied at the back of his neck. He raises his eyebrows and tilts his chin, up and down, to ask "what do you want?" He has much to do at the altar and has no time to waste.

The man steadies himself by placing his hand on the doorframe and smiles back, unperturbed. "I am here to seek an audience with His Holiness Lam Ngawang Chhoejé," the visitor declares. He is apparently oblivious to the austere atmosphere inside the *lhakhang* where a number of lamas are seated on raised cushions, talking in soft tones. He burps into the back of his hand and looks up at the *kongyer* who is standing at the raised doorway of the *lhakhang*. His breath reeks of *ara*. He smiles again, showing a set of strong unbrushed teeth.

"You can't meet Rinpoche," explains the monk, pushing the bandana down with his chin. "He's busy with the high lamas who are here to discuss tomorrow's *wang* (blessing ceremony). Go join the devotees out there and wait."

Outside, the crowd is gathering. Hundreds of people are arriving for the *tshewang* (long life blessings) scheduled for the next day, the auspicious 10th day of the 10th month. They are laying their clothes on the ground to reserve space as close to the monastery as possible to be close to the *Lam* the next morning. Tomorrow there will be thousands more arriving.

"No I don't think the lamas are really busy discussing the *wang*," says the visitor. "They are planning to raise funds tomorrow for the extension of the monastery." He grins at the *kongyer*.

Annoyed by the insolence of this obviously intoxicated man, the monk raises his voice. "I don't know how you got past the gate but I think it's time that you went back right now. If you have come for the *wang*, be there tomorrow."

Hearing their voices two other monks appear beside the *kongyer*. "Don't waste your time, *Lopon Kongyer*," says the older monk. "You have too much to do. The *tormas* are not even ready. You (addressing the visitor) get out of here."

The third monk, the youngest of the three, whispers to the other two. "I think this man is related to Rinpoche. Better check with Rinpoche before we kick him out." He disappears into the monastery.

The visitor steps further into the alcove. "I think it is funny that people are sitting out there praying to the lamas who are actually talking business. Do you think a bigger monastery will give better blessings?" He laughs.

Before the two monks can reply, the young monk returns and whispers to them. The *kongyer* turns to the visitor. "You can go in but be brief because Rinpoche has no time to waste," he says with obvious reluctance. "Take your shoes off," he adds sharply as the visitor moves towards the inner door.

The visitor kicks off his weather-beaten muddy shoes, picks them up, and walks towards the shoe rack lined with the bright brocade-covered boots of the lamas.

"No, not there," says the *kongyer*. "You, stranger, do not seem to know your place. Your dirty shoes cannot be placed with those of the lamas."

Still smiling, the visitor looks around the room. He notices a beam of the late afternoon sun coming through a half–open window. "All right, then, I'll leave it here." He walks towards the sunbeam, and casually places his shoes on the shaft of light. The pair of old shoes sit on the beam of sunlight. He looks at the monks and laughs.

Totally stunned, the three monks stare at the shoes sitting on the shaft of sunlight. They look at the visitor who is walking towards them, unsteady on his feet, a calm smile on his face. They quickly step back and prostrate on the floor as the unkempt visitor, Lam Drukpa Kuenley, walks through the door.

He walks towards the four lams who are sitting on thick cushions on the floor, facing each other, each with a *chhoedrom* in front of him. On the *choedroms* are cups of tea and baskets of snacks. He sits on the floor, beside Lam Ngawang Chhoejé. "So how much is it going to cost to make your *lhakhang* bigger?" Drukpa Kuenley asks his brother. He laughs. "Do you think you can raise it from your poor devotees tomorrow?"

Lam Ngawang Chhoejé looks at his brother, an exasperated expression on his face. The monks are all dressed in red gowns and tunics. As recognised trulkus, they wear a yellow band on their sleeves and collars. Two of the other lams look at the uninvited visitor, not hiding their irritation. The third and oldest lam is calmly shaping small animals out of rice dough. He has a number of rice balls in front of him and has already made three extremely life-like, beautifully poised, figures of deer.

"Kuenley," the youngest lam suddenly turns to him. "This is Lopon Tashi, a master in liturgical studies. Look at how the deer look like they are about to walk. We lams have to learn some things in the monastery you know. Would you like to try one?" he reaches over, picks up a ball of rice, and offers it to Drukpa Kuenley. The smile on his face seems to say that he expected to make a fool out of Kuenley.

"Of course I cannot do that," says Drukpa Kuenley. "I like to practice my skills on women, not on rice balls." He laughs. He is the only one laughing. Then Drukpa Kuenley takes the rice ball and throws it towards the door of the lhakhang. The ball of rice flies in an arc and lands on the floor. As soon as it touches the floor it turns into a live deer that stands up and walks out of the door.

The four lams sit shocked. A number of monks in the room prostrate on the floor.

Drukpa Kuenley gets up. "Actually I just came to say goodbye to my brother," he says. "I am leaving tomorrow for Bhutan where the girls are beautiful and the *chhang* tastes so good."

A Tiger's Tale

My jaws ache. I feel an agonising pain at the roots of my incisors with every bite as I tear mouthfuls of flesh from the carcass. Chewing the meat is agony. The searing pain shoots up to my skull. I rest every now and then to let the pain ease. It is torturous. Yet I must eat. I am hungry.

I look up. A human is standing on the stone wall in front of me, about 20 feet away. There are others around him but this one is clearly a leader of men. I look at him. Our eyes meet. I know he is not an ordinary human. This human conveys an aura of compassion.

*∗∗

I used to be a tiger. I was a proud specimen of one of the most dramatic animals that have ever roamed the earth. In my prime, weighing 300 kilogrammes, measuring 10 feet from my nose to my tail, I was a beautiful balance of lithe, grace, valour, and power. For 10 years I was one of the biggest and strongest beasts that walked the jungles of Bhutan.

I was born somewhere on the flat grasslands of Manas from where Bhutan's majestic mountain ranges rise and tower over the earth. It was on these vast plains that my mother taught me to walk, run, and hunt. I learnt to stalk small calves that strayed away from their mothers, and then small animals like hares, goats, and deer.

I learnt to use every blade of grass, shrub, stone and tree as camouflage to get close to my prey. As I grew older a deep thrill would take hold of my entire being as I unleashed my tensed muscles to spring into a charge, leap on my prey, and sink my teeth into its neck. As my body became increasingly muscular I had enough power to go after larger and faster animals. I had to. I had to eat.

My mother chased me away when I was 18 months old. I was free… free to survive. I was alone. The tropical jungles of Manas had many enemies. I had to kill or be killed. As a young tiger I would starve to death if I got injured and couldn't hunt. Human scientists will tell you that more than 30 out of 100 juvenile tigers perish in their first year. Another 17 percent of the survivors will die in the second year. I was among 20 out of every 100 tigers that live to become full adults.

By the time I was two years old I had the stealth, speed and strength to bring down cows, buffalos, camels, dogs, elephant and rhino calves, donkeys, goats, pigs and to break their necks with my jaws. When I turned four years old I was the ultimate predator. I often brought down 1,000 kilogramme animals. I would walk 15 to 20 kilometres at night and rest during the day. I had to kill once a week and eat about 100 kilogrammes of meat over three days.

The tragic irony was that, as strong and ferocious as I was, I belonged to a species facing extinction. I was one of an estimated 6,000 Royal Bengal Tigers left in South Asia and may be about 10,000 in 28 countries.

***

We had fallen victim to a meaner predator. Most tigers live in Asia. So do most humans. And 80 to 90 percent of Asians live off the land. So the natural habitat we used to share is consumed by settlements, agriculture, over-grazing, logging, roads, dams, mines, railways, tea, coffee and rubber plantations, fires… In South Asia we are also competing with a species called militants.

The wily human is the greatest threat to all animals, and to nature itself. Humans have been hunting the tiger for centuries. Man has used all his ingenuity to destroy everything around him and, in the process, himself. He has designed an incredible variety of traps to catch or kill the tiger. He uses nets, pits, baits, arrows, poisons, spears, electric fences.

Kings and nobility used to ride on the backs of elephants to hunt us. Modern man uses all the discoveries of science and technology to snare the tiger, as cubs and adults. When men invented the gun, in the west, they rushed to Asia to kill the tiger. These western maharajas shot the tiger from vehicles, using flashlights and sights.

The idea was to prove that they are rich, courageous, and virile. Hunting the tiger became a grand sport to prove their bravery. They write stories of dangerous encounters with the tigers to convince others of their courage. They take photographs with dead tigers. They mount tiger heads and hung tiger skins on their walls.

We are hunted for our teeth, bones, skin, claws. Our body parts are used as ingredients for medicines and as aphrodisiacs all over Asia. The image of the tiger is used to promote beer, gasoline, paint, cereals, computer software.

***

I was eventually forced to leave Manas because of human encroachment. For me personally this proved to be a blessing in disguise. I moved into Bhutan.

By the turn of the century about 150 Royal Bengal Tigers, including 70 to 80 adults, were living in Bhutan. Pushed out of our sub-tropical habitat, we moved through the temperate forests, climbing over 4,000-metre mountain passes. The steep and rugged terrain and the cold was uncomfortable at first. But we were better off than our kind in places like Siberia.

I had it good here. Nature existed in its purest state. My new hunting ground ranged from the sub tropical broadleaf forests close to sea level to the open Alpine ranges beyond the tree-line. I roamed over 11,000 square kilometres of rich forest hunting wild boar, deer, black bear, sambhar, serow, yaks, mules, horses, sheep, goats, and takin.

Other tigers kept out of my way. For 10 years no tiger would dare encroach into my hunting ground. I had my own territory to hunt. No tiger would dare go near my three tigresses. I had the potency to make my tigresses roar in ecstacy, sometimes 50 times a day.

***

Why was I fortunate to end up in Bhutan? Because this land is different. This is a land that has defied time. The people are different. The people have preserved human culture and mystique. They are not consumed by materialism.

This is a land where the aura of myth is alive. The people will not utter the word "tiger" because it carries too much power. I am an element of their culture. I am one of their four protector animals. I eat their animals but am accepted for my worth according to the laws of nature.

The Bhutanese people also understand that a living tiger is worth more than a dead one. Tigers look after forests. We protect water-soil resources. We are the apex of the food chain. We are a part of the eco system and an element in the habitat that humans need. We are important for man's own future on the planet.

The Bhutanese have real values. In 1957 they banned hunting to prevent the extinction of the tiger, long before other humans recognised the tiger as an endangered species. Their laws say that tigers should not be killed even if their livestock is attacked. The government imposes fines between Nu. 30,000 and Nu. 600,000 and imprisons people for killing tigers.

As people started losing more livestock to predators the government started a compensation fund in 2003 and, by 2004, had paid Nu. 3.48 million as compensation for loss of livestock.

Scientists predict that Bhutan's tiger landscape could become one of the world's most significant tiger habitat.

Bhutanese understand that a land without tigers has no magic.

***

But Bhutan, too, is changing. It is becoming like the others.

I generally avoided human habitats and humans although this was not always possible in Bhutan where people live with the forests. As I roamed the ridges above human habitat I looked down on rapid changes over the years.

The people are leaving their beautiful natural forests and building artificial habitats. The fields and forests have given way to concrete buildings. They used to build monasteries. Now they are building hotels. Like other Asian cities the Bhutanese capital is becoming crowded and noisy.

The landscape is changing rapidly. Looking down from Tango the valley is often covered by smog, dust, and smoke, the clear river is murky brown after it passes the city. The Bhutanese people used to be a part of nature. They do not know the forests any more. They used to take what they needed. Now they take what they can sell.

Men and women were fearless and strong. They walked for miles. They laughed and sang. They were special humans. Now they sit in concrete buildings all day. They fight among themselves. They used to seek happiness. Now they seek power.

Modern Bhutan is losing compassion. Why does Bhutan want to be like other countries in the region? Have they not seen what is happening?

And, sadly, the people think its progress.

***

"A tiger caught" – *Kuensel*, 5/11/2005

> Farmers in Tsaphey village in Haa dzongkhag are breathing easy after a male Royal Bengal Tiger which killed four animals in the village was sedated and caged on November 3.
> It was the fourth animal that the tiger killed in 20 days.
> "That was the second kill in four days," said Ugyen Lham who had lost a jersey cow three days earlier.
> Farmers and forestry officials had kept vigil during the night the tiger killed the mare. "We saw it attacking a neighbour's pig sty and didn't sleep the whole night," said

Dorji. "But before we knew what happened, it had killed my mare."

Tsaphey is about 2,670 meters above the sea level. Dr. Sangay Wangchuk, Nature Conservation Division's joint director, said that the tiger in Tsaphey had come prowling for easy prey. "The tiger is old, weak and cannot hunt its natural prey," he said. "It came looking for easier prey like domestic animals which are not adapted to running away from predators like tigers."

NCD's tiger expert, Tiger Sangay, added that the tiger had lost most of its claws, both canine teeth in the left jaw, and it's paws were infected. The specialist estimates the tiger to be more than 15 years old.

Meanwhile, NCD is building a temporary enclosure in Taba to house the tiger. Officials said that the tiger is too weak to be released in the wild. "If we let it go it will die because it is too weak to hunt," Tiger Sangay said.

***

Yes that is me, now chewing on this old horse. I was once the ultimate land predator, able to snap the necks of adult yaks. My tigresses would quiver with anticipation when I approached them. Now even small animals do not bother to run away from me. I am chased out of my territory by a younger male. I am forced to look for domestic animals that cannot run away. I will attack humans if they are alone. I am old. It is a time of agony and shame.

***

The human on the wall is Bhutan's King. He does not need to feed his ego by killing a tiger. He is clearly a Bodhisattva. His expression softens as I looked at him. "Look after this old tiger," he commands.

***

I do not live long with the Bhutanese people. My time has come. But, during these last few days, my faith in the human race is a little restored. There is kindness here. There is hope. At the same time I despair at what I see. Just as there are more tigers pacing small cages than wild forests the Bhutanese people, too, are an endangered species.

A Legend That Lives

It is a fine day in the year 747 AD. The Guru wakes up in his celestial palace and stretches his massive frame. It is time to subdue the restless spirits in this land that is destined to be home to the profound philosophies that the Buddha realised. This pure land must be prepared for the challenges of the future, perils that human society will create for itself.

Yeshe Tshogyal - the Guru's queen, disciple, yogini - offers him the three layers of patterned silk garments symbolising discipline, mediation, and wisdom. She adjusts them over his white silk undergarment. She places a thick maroon robe over his powerful shoulders as he pulls on his long boots.

Yeshe Tshogyal then transforms herself into the emanation of the mythical flying tigress. Her sleek and graceful body spreads itself in elegant anticipation as the Guru dons the lotus cap, its vajra and eagle feather soaring up towards higher realms. He holds the vajra sceptor of skilful means high in his right hand and the skull bowl of wisdom in his left hand. His staff sits on the crook of his left arm. The air shakes with vibrance as the Guru mounts the tigress. The two merge into the atmosphere.

The flight is magical. The Guru and the yogini are instantly transported to an inaccessible cave in western Bhutan. The deep crevice of this cave cuts into a sheer 800-metre rock face, 2,950 metres above sea level. The cliff is surrounded by a giant inhospitable ravine that itself resembles an enormous cavern fitted deep into the mountainside, defying human entry. The entire atmosphere is tense with the mood of the feared spirits that haunt the region. Their negative energy drapes the valleys below, stifling all life forms.

Suddenly the cave, then the ravine, then the valley, is filled with the awesome presence of Dorji Drollo. His wrathful form is a fearsome maroon. His curly dark yellow hair, orange moustache, beard and eyebrows wave wildly. Three bloodshot eyes shoot powerful beams of light. His upper fangs bite down on the lower lip. The right hand is raised high, holding a gold vajra, ready to strike. His left hand thrusts out a phurba of meteorite iron. His bone earrings and necklace of severed heads thrash about. His coloured robes flap around him. The entire body is surrounded by a halo of red and orange flames, burning with compassion. His ferocious presence is overwhelming. A silent roar fills the gorge and reverberates over the mountains.

Within moments, the energies of the restless spirits are harnessed by the power of the Guru's divine benevolence. He binds them into submission and tames them into the service of Buddhism. The most feared of the vanquished local deities, Singye Samdrup, becomes the guardian of Taktshang (the Tiger's Lair). The entire countryside is enveloped in a sense of harmony. It is the end of confusion and ignorance. It is the beginning of realisation.

Taktshang thus becomes one of the most sacred sites on earth.

***

Sitting on the edge of the vertical precipice, opposite the Taktshang Monastery, I avoid looking down into the gorge. Following the contour of the cliff into its abysmal depths makes me dizzy. But, when I look across at the lhakhang, Bhutanese history comes alive in my mind. This tantric mythology is real. This forebodingly beautiful ravine is home to powerful legends. Deities subdued wild spirits here. Saints and lamas sat in tranquil meditation. Yogis sang their realisations. Scholars conceived volumes of transmissions. Tertons discovered treasures. Historical leaders crafted their visions here.

This dramatic monument to Buddhism drew spiritual giants like Milarepa, Phadampa Sangye, Machi Labdoenma, Thangthong Gyalpo, and Zhabdrung Ngawang Namgyal. The figures that created Bhutanese history constructed the famed monastery. Representing the best of human architectural ingenuity this is an image that has been flashed around the world.

Taktshang's spirituality is overwhelming. So is my realisation that this kingdom is as dramatic as it was centuries ago. This Vajrayana kingdom, more than 1,000 years later, is suspended in that same realm.

***

Anim Choden practically lives in the clouds. The Zangto Pelri Lhakhang where she is in retreat is perched on a cliff edge high above the gorge opposite Taktshang. She has lived there for more than 20 years. She does not know her age but she knows that she is more than 60 years. She has no family. She never leaves the lhakhang. Apart from half a dozen hermitages scattered over the cliffs, she has no neighbours.

On April 19, 1998, the *kongyer* (caretaker) of the Zangto Pelri

Lhakang has gone down to Paro valley. She is alone. Sitting outside the lhakang, looking down at Taktshang, she thinks that the weather has gone crazy. The sun shines bright in the morning. At mid-day Taktshang is suddenly thrown into the shade of a dark cloud. The wind howls. There is a drizzle. Then there are snowflakes that do not rise or fall but swirl around. Then it is gone. Just before dusk the sun shines again.

It is about 7.00 pm that Anim Choden sees a tongue of flame from the central *lhakhang* of Taktshang. Then another from one of the front *lhakhangs*. The flames build into a giant volume of fire that covers the rockface. The huge roar of the inferno echoes up and down the ravine. She falls on her hands and knees. She screams, but the only sound that comes out of her throat are choked sobs.

Within hours a growing number of men from Paro valley gather opposite the Monastery. They watch in shock as the cruel blaze consumes the temples of Taktshang. Down in the valley people look helplessly up at the flames that throw a giant flickering shadow over them. Word goes around and people all over the country are strangely quiet that night. They share the anguish in silence. Overseas, photographs of Taktshang are quickly exchanged on the Internet. News is relayed by e-mail. The world hears about the calamity before the fire is out.

***

Passang: Berkeley, California

Hi... anyone online?

I'm sitting in the college library, depressed. Since I heard about the Taktshang fire yesterday, my senses have gone numb. My food tastes like mud. I can't focus on my classes. I even skipped the Bulls' match against the Lakers.

Thinking about it, the human dimension to this tragedy is profound. As an economics student I realise that economic successes really means nothing if we have no identity. And that the loss of heritage strikes at the roots of a nation's existence and identity. The real essence of the Bhutanese identity is our living heritage... our cultural and spiritual legacy.

It didn't strike me how special it is to be a Bhutanese until yesterday.

Dema: New York

Hey Passang,

No need to be so depressed. The most sacred sanctum of Taktshang is the cave where Guru Rinpoche meditated. That holy space cannot be burnt.

Come over to New York this weekend. We are having an *ema datshi* night to cheer ourselves.

Chencho: Geneva

Hi everyone... I spoke to my grandfather in Shaba. He is so upset... he believes this a bad omen. Our collective merit is lost and this signals the degeneration of society.

He thinks it is a shame for Parops. I'm ashamed because the only time I went to Taktshang was to pray for good exam results two years ago.

Sigay: Oakland

Don't worry, Chencho, I did the same. When I was studying in Semtokha I used to go every year to Talakha before the exams. The idea is that you pray for the presence of mind to work hard and get good results. You shouldn't be slack and expect good results just by offering *nyenda* (prayer).

Dago: New York

I agree with Passang.

I am an illegal migrant worker... now I'm wondering what the hell I'm doing here... a nobody... struggling from one kitchen to another.

Thanks to whoever uploaded the picture of Taktshang. It made me cry.

Dechen: Amsterdam

I went to Drukgyel High School. Taktshang was there all the time. I can't imagine driving by with no Taktshang up on the cliff.

Nancy: Nova Scotia

Did you know that Trungpa Rinpoche went to meditate at Taktshang in 1968? Rinpoche was so inspired by the spiritual power of Taktshang that he wrote this incredibly profound poem. I'm posting a few lines here:

At glorious Taktshang, in the cave
Which can accommodate everything
Samsara and nirvana both
The heretics and bandits of hope and fear
Are subdued and all experiences
Are transformed into crazy wisdom
Is not this your doing, O Dorje Trolo?

Tashi: Bangalore

I have never been to Taktshang. I took this precious *nye* for granted and now its gone. I am thinking of all the *nyes* that we have and am determined to visit all of them as soon as I get home.

Gedon: Bangkok

Hi... I study in Bangkok which must be the busiest and messiest city in the world. I am sitting here and wondering... If our Buddhist *nyes* are meant to help all sentient beings how can our chhortens and lhakhangs in Bhutan help people in Bangkok?

Toni: France

Hello... I am a French student of Mahayana Buddhism. From what my Rinpoche taught me this is how I understand it. It is a bit like acupuncture. Your body is a system of nerves, veins, arteries, muscles, bones, etc.. They work in coordination to form the whole. That's why, in acupuncture, if you are suffering pain somewhere on your body the acupuncturist does not stick the needle where it hurts but in a strategic spot where there could be a block or trauma that causes pain down the line. There are special areas of the body which are critical centres that have an impact on other parts.

Now think of the world itself – even the universe - as a system of energies in a fine balance. Enlightened Rinpoches recognise critical spots that are like nerve centres that affect the whole. You Bhutanese call them *nyes*. Building a chhorten or lhakhang on such a spot is like sticking an acupuncture needle into a human body. It benefits the entire universal flow of energy and maintains the right balance. That is why Taktshang is important for the world.

Sonam: Sydney

Bhutan is an abode of the Vajrayana spirit. The fire was a powerful lesson in impermanence and it is a rude awakening. I think its time for serious introspection.

What does it mean? I fear that we are getting more and more absorbed with material development. Has the degeneration of values in our society created the need for a regeneration of values? Perhaps the tragedy calls for a new awareness of our legacies and for a new determination in all of us...

Dorji: Kyoto

Japan, one of the most modern and economically successful countries, is trying to cling to its traditions. All their sacred heritage are safeguarded and even traditional singers are insured as national treasures.

Japan often has disasters like earthquakes and floods that destroy buildings, including monuments. Therefore they have a team of traditional artisans to restore these buildings. It seems like this is one way, although a back-handed advantage, to preserve our 13 arts and crafts. As Taktshang is re-built a new generation of Bhutanese craftsmen will hone the skills that their forefathers kept alive over the centuries.

Gyem: Delhi

My uncle, Ap Tobgye, was the *kongyer* of Taktshang for three years. He thinks the fire was a blessing in disguise. He says that the old lhakhang would have lasted just another few years. Now they will build a new lhakhang.

***

For several weeks after the Taktshang fire I listened regularly to a sitar piece by the blues guitarist, Ry Cooder, called "A Meeting By The River". The haunting notes of the sitar stirred graphic images in my mind and the moods that we were all going through. The meditative beginning was the old Taktshang perched serenely on the cliff. As the music built up to a beautiful high pitch crescendo it was Anim Choden, high up on the peak, trying to scream, her tears expressing the anguish of every Bhutanese. As the notes wound down it was the pensive aftermath of the fire, a time for reflection.

***

On April 23, 1998, King Jigme Singye Wangchuck climbs up to the charred remains of Taktshang. He recovers a number of the precious *nangtens* (inner treasures) from the sacred cave, known as the *dubkhang*. Standing on the ruins of history, His Majesty the King assures the gathering of shocked devotees that a fire might burn the physical structures but that it cannot destroy the spiritual aura of Taktshang. The King issues the command that no effort should be spared to restore Taktshang Monastery, in traditional architectural splendour, to its former glory.

***

The reconstruction of Taktshang Monastery was declared a "Bhutanese effort". Thousands of people, many of whom had not even thought about visiting Taktshang in the past, contributed cash, kind, and labour. People, young and old, volunteered to help at the reconstruction site, some carrying stones and construction material as a symbol of Buddhist practice.

I saw that a destroyed Taktshang, in many ways, touched more people than the old monastery had done. Within days of the fire letters poured into the country from all corners of the world. The global community grieved the destruction of an important human heritage. It was a reminder of how many people had visited Taktshang and astonishing how many people considered it the most memorable experience in their lives.

It is not just saints who are inspired by this *nye*. "I am not a spiritual person but, when I reached Taktshang, I cried," said a Singapore businesswoman. "Climbing up to Taktshang was my life's achievement," said an American actor. "Taktshang inspired Prince Charles to paint," said a British diplomat. "This is the most sacred place on earth," said a Japanese photographer. "Anyone who comes to Taktshang on pilgrimage goes back a changed person," said the monk caretaker.

***

I am back on the sheer precipice on March 26, 2005, for the consecration of the new *lhakhang*. It dawns on me that Taktshang is not just a monument. The legend lives on. The mythology is no less dramatic today than it was in 747 AD.

The spirituality is vibrant in the *dubkhang*, which is the most sacred sanctum of Taktshang. The 10 main temples and numerous sacred spaces around this sanctified cave have been rebuilt in a blend of traditional architecture at its best and modern engineering techniques.

In the process of construction the Bhutanese people saw history re-enacted. At the helm was a Monarch who seemed destined to restore the faith and revive a fresh spiritual energy in his people. Just as Zhabdrung Ngawang Namgyal had done in the 17th century King Jigme Singye Wanghuck, believed to be a reincarnation of the Zhabdrung, constructed a magnificent monument around this sacred *nye* of Guru Rinpoche. The consecration of the *lhakhang* is conducted by none other than Gyalse Tenzin Rabgye the reincarnation of the great fourth Desi, Tenzin Rabgye, who completed the first monastery for the Zhabdrung three hundred years ago.

***

That day the chants of the Dorji Phurpa (Vajrakilaya, the embodiment and emanation of the activities of all Buddhas) in the Sungjoenma Lhakhang seems to echo through the centuries. As King Jigme Singye Wangchuck leads the ceremonial line of monks, the royal family, government leaders, international representatives and people from all walks of life up the steep path to Taktshang, it is a vivid scene from the Guru's own realm.

***

As the sounds of the consecration ceremony waft up the ravine, Anim Choden weeps again. This time she cries tears of joy.

When Fortune Smiles

Why do we sometimes write about ourselves and expect people to be interested? Because our stories are usually not about ourselves. It is about everything, and everyone, around us.

My story begins as a classic cliché. In January, 2005, at Paddington station in London, I was robbed of my passport, tickets, and money the day before I was supposed to leave the country. At that time it seemed like a major disaster. Over the months it evolved into a great human interest story.

At about noon on January 19, 2005, I arrived at Paddington station, completing the last leg of a week-long visit to the United Kingdom. Travelling through the English countryside had been a strangely nostalgic experience. At boarding school in northern India, from 1965 to 1975, I was brought up on textbooks called English Readouts and storybooks based in England. The images of green fields where brown and white cows grazed, church steeples rising above red village roofs, and farmers in tweed jackets driving tractors had been foreign to me but now came alive, 30 years later, as I looked out of the train window.

I arrived at Paddington with a feeling of satisfaction that, not only had I held a series of productive meetings with newspaper editors over the past few days, I had used this last train ride to type all my notes into my laptop. I clicked it closed not long before I reached the station, and before the battery ran out. I did not know then that it was my luck that had run out.

At Paddington the man who was supposed to take me to the hotel was not there. Actually I did not need the ride. My hotel was so close that it would have taken me a few minutes and less than five pounds to get there by taxi. But I was expecting some papers. Since this was my last day I expected the escort to have some documents for me, including a copy of the BBC Charter that I had requested. So I decided to wait for half an hour at the station. Once I had my papers I could truly wrap up the visit, spend the afternoon with a friend, and head home.

***

"Wait, don't tell me what happened," said a British friend, months later, when I started telling him my story. "Let me guess. You sat down, put your bag next to you, and moments later, it was gone."

The place was an innocent looking sushi bar in the middle of the station. It was brightly lit and not too crowded. I sat on a stool facing the platform where my escort should have been waiting for me, waving a placard with my name on it. After eating two small plates of green soya beans I gave up and reached for my bag. It was gone. My laptop on which it was sitting and my overnight roller bag near the stool were still there.

**

Now, like many other people, I've always believed that when you get robbed your immediate response is despair and anger, in that order. I found out that it is actually shock and then a slow realisation of what has happened. Despair and anger come later, much later.

The instant the manager of the sushi bar saw my face he knew that I had been robbed. He knew because had seen many people robbed at the sushi bar. Paddington station reports an average of seven robberies a day. But the people working at the bar have never thought about warning their customers. I cannot prove it but I believe my bag was taken when a waitress attracted my attention to explain the sushi menu.

Then, dear readers, I would like to share with you the astounding fact that, when you get robbed at Paddington station, the police do not want to know about it. On my insistence the manager of the sushi bar rang the police several times but they refused to come. But they eventually revealed that I could report the robbery to the Paddington station police.

***

The small window on Platform One was manned by a police officer, about six feet tall, with oval-shaped brown-rimmed glasses and a drooping brown mustache. Leaning on the counter inside the widow, he filled out a slip of paper which said "passport, ticket, money stolen", signed it, and handed it to me through a small hole at the counter. When I asked him what next, he seemed surprised. "You take that and do what you have to with your bank if you've lost your credit card." When I asked him what he was going to do about the robbery he was shocked. "What do you expect me to do?" I had no ready answer to that. What do we expect policemen to do when we get robbed?

The afternoon had more in store. I walked back to the sushi bar where I had left by roller bag with the manager. He told me that a couple sitting on the other side of my bag had seen the entire robbery. They had watched me being robbed and had not said a word. The man had given the manager his name and telephone number so that he could describe the thief to the police if they wanted the information. The police, of course, didn't.

I ran back to the police window with the telephone number. Another police officer, about the same height but heavier, clean-shaven with black curly hair, informed me that the previous officer had gone home. I explained the situation and thrust the paper with the eye-witness' number through the window, excited with this clue. This officer was as shocked as the previous one that he was expected to do something. "Look," he said. "If anyone hands the bag to us we'll call you." He returned the paper with the witness' number on it.

After pacing the station for another half an hour I returned to the police window. There was a third officer at the window, about five feet, 10 inch tall with a beer gut that hung over his belt. Darker in complexion than the other two he spoke with a slight accent that I could not place. I explained the situation again. "I really need to understand this," I told him. "I am not able to understand why the police will do nothing to help someone who has been robbed of everything. A witness wants to talk and you don't want to talk to him."

What he said next was more astounding than ever. "Look mate, we don't need to talk to the witness. There are cameras all over the station. There's one directly above the sushi bar. The whole robbery is on film". I felt a flood of relief. "When will you get him?" I still had time to go home. I would be grateful for my passport and tickets and thumb drive. Forget the money, the papers, and the address book.

"We won't," he said. "We have no access to the tapes. The cameras are controlled by another branch of police." This, according to a taxi driver who took me to my hotel, was why the public should not expect help at Paddington station. The railway police are the lowest of the low in the police hierarchy so they take out their frustrations on the people.

The police officer decided to console me with the information that others had suffered worse fates here at Paddington. Only days ago an Australian had been robbed of a bag that contained critical medication for his heart and a British lawyer had lost a laptop that had the details of a seven million pound case he had been working on for two years. I found it difficult to find consolation in the fact that they had done nothing about these either.

***

Murphy, of Murphy's law, knew what he was talking about. Suddenly everything that could go wrong, seemed to go wrong. I had been accompanied by an escort everywhere during my week-long visit and was robbed the only time one did not show up. It was Friday afternoon and the airline office closed for the next two days. I was introduced to the world of call centres. Every time I rang to check on my air tickets I was speaking to a different person in Manila, Mumbai, or Delhi. So I called the Thai office in Kolkota, India, to issue my tickets in London.

When I eventually had a passport sent to me, DHL misplaced it. DHL has a great policy. If a customer has a complaint against DHL the only place he can complain is to DHL. In the next few days I heard hours of recorded messages and spoke to more people at call centres in India and in the Philippines as I tried to find my passport. The Internet has done wonders. It has brought people of the world together on a shared platform. I realise that we talk much more but say much less. It is at such a stage the frustration sets in.

***

There is no shortage of advice when you get robbed. "You must be careful," a lot of people advised me. Some reiterated their faith in me: "You of all people getting robbed?" So it was a relief when a British woman friend simply expressed her view of the inertia of the Paddington police. "The bastards. There are hundreds of them to give you parking tickets. But not one to help people who are robbed."

Another friend was more cynical. "They probably entertain themselves watching us being robbed," she said. "There goes Sleazy Sam, let's see how long before he gets that Japanese tourist. They might have been betting among themselves on how long it would be before he got you."

***

Mustering all the objectivity that I could I understood that the British police must be short-staffed. In this day and age, there are terrorists to run after. Like the couple that watched me getting robbed, I learned that British citizens are advised by their police not to interfere when they see a crime being committed. They might get hurt.

But it is difficult to accept that the entire police force will allow helpless travelers to be subjected to extreme emotional agony while they wait for an Al Qaeda attack. I concluded, in all sincerity, that there is something fundamentally wrong when an entire robbery is on police film, and the police know the thieves, and the victim is not helped. There is something wrong when the average citizen sees a robbery makes no attempt to warn the victim, leave alone intervene.

Thus I lapsed into moments of profundity. I felt a surge of relief that, today, in "under-developed" Bhutan, I would not be robbed if

I left my bag in a restaurant. It is still common that, when foreign visitors forget a camera or other personal belongings anywhere in the country, they eventually find it. Well, perhaps not any more in the capital where the most developed people live.

So is this the price of development?

***

Every story has an end. Mine ended in the perspectives of my mother's friend, a 90-year old Buddhist nun I met after the trip. I was born in the year of the rooster and, according to Bhutanese belief, I was at my most vulnerable because it was the year of the rooster. That is why Bhutanese people perform special ceremonies, when their animal sign comes around, to ward off misfortune.

"You lucky man," she told me when she heard my story. "Your bad luck was robbed. You were not harmed. All the negative energy was stolen from you with that bag."

A great weight was lifted from my mind.

A Bhutanese In Japan

The *on-sen* - hot spring bath, Japanese style – is a great Japanese experience. Apart from the wonderful bath it depicts the Japanese sense of aestheticism in all its finesse as well as the uncompromising cultural sensitivity of Japanese society. I learnt that during my first visit to Japan, the hard way.

I was used to Bhutan's hot springs where men, women, and children of all shapes and sizes soak in various stages of dress and undress. Some people bathe stark naked, some bathe in their underwear, others use shorts and petticoats. People come from far and wide to soak in the pools that are believed to have the therapeutic value. Nomads, tourists, travelers, and people suffering from various illnesses camp for days by the pools, immersed in the hot sulfur water all day. At the most popular hot springs in the northern district of Gasa the largest of six pools is reserved for mules that love a hot soak after days on the strenuous mountain trails.

***

As a worthy journalist I had done my research and learnt that one thing you do not do is go to a Japanese public bath with your clothes on. You bathe stark naked after going through long-established norms of washing yourself. The etiquette is so important that Japanese society is seriously offended by ill-bred *gaijin* (foreigners) who do not understand this. So I was more than prepared.

I went to my first bath, thrilled to look like a Samurai warrior in my *yukata* (summer kimono). After confirming, discreetly, that the other men undressed completely and walked naked to the bath area, I strolled confidently through a bamboo partition into a large room where all the men were preparing for the baths.

I was standing, straight and proud, in the middle of the room when I noticed that every man in that room held a small towel with which he modestly covered his manhood. (I learnt later that I should have brought the *tenugui*, an essential article for the bath, from my room.) It was one of the unforgettable moments of my life, standing there, among a crowd of naked men, the only man without a towel.

***

I returned to Japan five years later, a much wiser self-professed public intellectual. Okada-san, my 70-year old absent-minded friend, who had worked as a senior volunteer in Bhutan, picked me up at the airport on August 30, 2004. After we eventually figured out where he had parked his car and delayed traffic at the toll gate because Okada-san lost his ticket, we missed the highway leading into Tokyo. Tired after a sleepless flight I told Okada-san to take his time and fell asleep in the car. Some 30 minutes later I woke up to find myself alone in the car which was rolling down the slope. I managed to pull the hand brake and learnt, when Okada-san came running after the car, that he had forgotten to pull the brake when he went out to ask for directions.

I also learned that Okada-san was leaving the country again on a volunteer mission to Costa Rica. I thought I'd tease my friend. "You mean your wife doesn't mind you leaving again so soon?" "No," he said, "she's very happy." I thought Okada-san was getting witty. In the following weeks I was to learn why his wife was genuinely pleased to get him out of the country.

It was not just Okada-san. I knew a number of senior Japanese volunteers in Bhutan and visited them in Kobe and Hokkaido. They were incredibly wonderful hosts who accompanied me all day sightseeing and, in Hokkaido, drove me long distances to look at plant life. I was genuinely apologetic for wasting their time but the response was consistent: "No problem. We are free. We have nothing to do."

It was not a happy freedom. My friends, post-war babies now retired, were dealing somewhat helplessly with the twilight years of their lives, alone. Apart from more than 30,000 Japanese who are over 100 years, there are several million unemployed senior citizens. Shibuya-san in Kobe explained to me that many of them had never spent much time at home during their working lives so their wives found their daily presence difficult to deal with. That was why couples were divorcing late in their lives.

***

I had been invited to attend the Asia Leadership Fellowship Programme, a gathering of academics, journalists, and activists from Asia. It was a two-month seminar to understand Japan, and Asia, better and to be a part of a growing network of Asian intellectuals. What I saw was some of the anguish behind the facade of an incredibly successful and wealthy society that we see from an Asian perspective. And it was the Asian-ness of this perspective that helped us understand the emotions that lie behind what western society likes to call the inscrutable face of Japan.

Hiroshima and Nagasaki invoke in the visitor memories of a war that is hard to come to terms with and the images are vivid in the Hiroshima atom bomb museum. History came agonisingly alive when we had dinner with an A-bomb survivor who had undergone surgery 27 times. Equally painful are the reminders of the atrocities committed by Japanese soldiers in east and southeast Asia. A senior Japanese scholar could not choke back the tears when he recapped the experience and apologised to our colleagues from China and the Philippines for the behaviour of his countrymen.

The mixture of distress and regret as well as the sensitivity of the topic itself were palpable when we met a writer who has literally torn apart the myth of the kamikaze pilots. She too was overwhelmed by emotion as she talked about what she had learnt from the diaries of the young pilots who had sacrificed their lives for their country. She appeared to share the suffering of those reluctant heroes during the last nights in their camps and the nightmares that preceded the solemn oaths that they took before their Emperor the next day.

We came across a deep discomfort when we discussed nationhood as it was symbolised by the Emperor, the national flag, and the national anthem. I picked up the distinct impression that these obvious symbols of the homeland were perceived to be tainted. The post-war generation of Japanese is not comfortable with history. Apart from Singapore, which has pragmatically chosen to bury the past, Japan continues to be confronted by its Asian neighbours for their "war crimes". And I do not think it helps that debate on the issue is generally avoided.

As I tried to meditate in the beautiful surroundings of the International House garden, it was difficult not to feel the weight of Japanese history.

***

I was sensitive to the nuances. I understood that there were some issues I should not confront. Although Japan widely acknowledged the fact that the aging population was a problem we were not supposed to ask women why they did not want children, or husbands in some cases. An interpreter squirmed when I asked her if she had children. A young Ainu artist gave us a lesson in Ainu art and ate dinner with us but it was rude to ask her, even academically, why she seemed to distance herself from other Ainu.

The dynamic head of a major corporation was quick to admit that Japanese corporations took too much of their employees' time and kept them away from their families. But even he was doing nothing about it and, as a Japanese journalist told me, young men like his son do not meet their parents because they come home after midnight and leave before daybreak for work.

***

Even as Japanese thinkers are beginning to question the quality of life in this rich society and the level of unhappiness of the people, I believe that Japan, as an Asian leader, deserves a better global image. Japan's international stature was assured mostly because of the large funds it contributed but poor communication mars its public face. Although this has been attributed to poor language I believe that culture, which prevents Japanese from holding open and forthright discussions, contributes to the impression that Japanese are "difficult" to deal with. An attitude problem also emerges, particularly when Japanese men deal with women.

The organisers of our seminar, the International House and Japan Foundation, gave us valuable exposure to some of the more unsavory aspects of Japanese society. This included the government's apparent discrimination against the Korean and Buraku minorities in Kyoto. A day visit showed the layers of tension as local Korean communities who were complaining about discrimination themselves rejected newer arrivals. In Hokkaido the Ainu culture has been reduced to a small museum and an enchanting restaurant where we – the chosen Asian public intellectuals – sang a Beatles' song with a sense of cultural cringe.

***

Of course I fell in love with Japan. The colours of October in Hokkaido will remain a permanent memory, now living in some small saplings that I nursed all the way back home. A drive through Niseko ski resort, a walk through the woods, a hot bath in the *on-sen*, and an elaborate traditional Japanese dinner washed down with warm *sake* and I was asking: "What have I done to deserve this?" I will not even attempt to describe Japanese food. How can you adequately describe the colours of the seasons being moulded into a *toraya* cake or the fragrance of fresh fish in a sushi lunch on the edge of the water in Otaru city?

I hit the karaoke scene in a big way. Microphone in hand, I sensed the thrill that makes Japanese men and women, who are generally subdued and quiet all day, sing and writhe with absolute abandon at night.

***

I was contemplating "Gross National Happiness", a development goal inspired by the King of Bhutan. But I found new meaning to happiness when I sat in an outdoor *on-sen* on Hachijo-jima island, half-way up the Hachijo-Jima-Fuji volcano, with a delicate pine and bamboo mixed forest in the background and the open Pacific in the front. And happiness turned into ecstacy when my wife joined me in a traditional *ryokan*, far down the coast of the Izu Peninsula, in a room filled with the aroma of fresh *tatami*.

***

With Bhutan poised on the edge of dramatic political change I was excited in a strangely nostalgic way by Japan's thinking during the Meiji restoration period after 1868. Japan and Bhutan seemed like two similar worlds, 150 years apart. With the advantage of hindsight, Bhutan decided that modernisation was not westernisation while Japan then opted to westernise, but some similarities are amazing.

Thousands of Japanese tourists come to Bhutan every year, their main reason being that Bhutan reminds them of what Japan must have once been like. For them it is a trip back into time. Both are Buddhist countries with a King and Emperor as symbols of unity. Bhutanese people are mistaken for Japanese and never for Chinese. But I had not been able to see any real connection in two countries that were, otherwise, poles apart.

I hit upon a clue. It was not in the research of scholars or in the historical libraries, but in uncanny similarities that I heard in a small noodle house in Azabu when we chatted over cups of hot *shochu* that tastes like our *ara*. When Japanese men introduce their wives to a friend or business partner they say, "Please meet my *gusai*," meaning my foolish or ugly wife. Bhutanese women say "My husband is a tsagay (idiot)." Although there is a gender difference here the intended social modesty is the same. I don't know of any other culture that does this. I also know that it is common in both cultures to lay out a major feast for a guest and apologise for "such a simple meal". To cap it all I learnt that Japanese men used to go "night hunting" for girls not so long ago. Bhutanese men still do it and we also call it "night hunting".

I believe that I received an insight into the real essence of the Japanese value system when I went to a four-hour *kabuki* play that everyone said would be boring. Set in a village school the story of a nobleman who sacrificed his son out of his love and loyalty for his king reduced me to tears. As a Bhutanese I could identify with this depth of human relationship and value.

A sadder similarity is that such nobility is now largely confined to mythology.

In recent years Japanese intellectuals and the Japanese government have taken an interest in Gross National Happiness as a higher goal for human development. I am excited about the growing interaction because, in many ways, Bhutan and Japan are two countries that represent opposite extremes.

Japanese society, as interpreted by its critics, has wealth and a fair share of unhappiness. Bhutan is financially poor but claims to be happy. It will be an interesting human experiment if the two societies seek a meeting point. Will we find out how we can both be rich and happy or will we end up being poor and unhappy?

THE ANSWER LIES BACK HOME

"What are you going to do in the Netherlands?" It was 6.00 am at Schiphol airport in Amsterdam on a June day in 1997. The unshaven immigration official squinted through the pages of my Bhutanese passport and, from the raised immigration podium, looked down on me with an expression that was as foreign as I felt.

It was exactly what I had been asking myself during a restless 12-hour flight from Bangkok. I was in the Netherlands as a part of a progressive and somewhat ambitious experiment to give more sensitivity and meaning to the relationship between rich and poor countries in the process that is politely called development cooperation.

Bhutan and the Netherlands were a part of a project called the Sustainable Development Agreement (SDA) initiated by the Dutch government. The idea was to make the development aid process a real sharing of experiences. We were trying to envision international aid being a two-way cooperation where the so-called developed countries, believe it or not, could also learn some lessons from the "poor".

As far as I could see there were very few people who had an understanding of this concept. There were some who thought they did. Others pretended they did. And the rest - the majority – did not care.

***

So I started making connections with people. For my first appointment I asked to meet a well-known Dutch journalist and author, hoping for an insight into the Dutch view of our small Himalayan kingdom. He declined, saying that he could recommend a colleague who knew much more than he did about Africa.

Obviously this was not going to be simple. I was not going to find an insight into humanity's problems so easily. In fact all I could see were the differences between two countries that seemed worlds apart in their geography, economies, cultures, and their values.

The differences were as dramatic as the contrast between the rugged contours of the world's highest mountain range and the manicured Dutch flatlands, much of it below sea level.

I could not help but be struck by a psychological distance between two societies at two ends of the economic spectrum, one enjoying economic success from very liberal trade policies, the other characterised by its efforts to preserve traditional Buddhist culture. The densely populated cities in this land of 14 million people was a stark contrast to the sparsely distributed 600,000 or so Bhutanese over rugged mountain terrain.

***

Sustainable development became a buzzword after the 1992 Earth Summit in Rio when nations made the commitment to look after the earth for their fellow men and for future generations.

SDA was born from such a noble thought. Accepting that the human population has equal rights to the natural elements in the atmosphere, developed countries must pay for emitting far more than their share of, say, Carbon Dioxide. They should, therefore, pay a country like Bhutan which contributes to the ecological balance by not producing poisonous gases.

Drawing from the Buddhist concept of interdependence among all sentient beings, where man and nature depend on each other, the Bhutanese have maintained a pristine environment. More than any other country, we had taken decisions to even sacrifice economic benefits to protect our environment for future generations. It is law in Bhutan that 60 percent of the country must remain under forest cover.

The Netherlands recognised Bhutan as an example of a sustainable society. In what was called a "debt for nature swap" SDA had even paid US$5.00 million to free Bhutan of loans and enabled the kingdom to save large stretches of forests by closing down a plywood and wood manufacturing plant.

***

Noble concepts do not seem to go far in practice. It was difficult to see industrialised countries translating Rio's ambitions from rhetoric into reality. "The progress since the Rio meeting has not been enormous." This was one of the greatest understatements of the century when I met the dynamic Dutch minister for development aid and a pioneer of SDA, Jan Pronk, in the Hague, five years after Rio. Not long after our meeting SDA itself was scuttled by the next minister for development co-operation.

It seemed unlikely that the United States, for example, would give up that second or third family car to share the concern for a depleting ozone layer. Mr. Al Gore had to lose the elections to think up the idea of looking at the "Inconvenient Truth" of an ecologically destabilising world. Years later I was to meet the governor of California, Mr. Arnold Schwarzenegger, who believes that every 16 year-old American youth should have a car.

So sustainability remains a dilemma. The concept is not criticised but faces skepticism. It is not a failure, but neither is it a success. It has made progress, but there are no visible results. Global efforts in issues like sustainability and climate change has not achieved much beyond the symbolism of large meetings.

⁎

So where does a Bhutanese man stand in this major human dilemma? Led by what must have been intuition I walked along the famous De Wallen in Amsterdam to look at an incredible variety of prostitutes (live and real) displayed behind glass windows and ended up in front of a Tibetan restaurant. More curious than hungry I opened the door and saw that the only customers were a Bhutanese woman friend, her Dutch husband, and a Dutch man who had just returned from Bhutan. They were eating *momos*.

After many bottles of beer and dozens of *momos* made by a chef who was Chinese, not Tibetan, we all agreed that the search for sustainability had to begin, and end, in Bhutan. The answers lay, more than the Rio Declaration or the Kyoto Protocol, in Gross National Happiness.

***

I was not long in the Netherlands before I understood that differences, between people and places, is a good basis to learn about each other. We make connections as humans and, through this experience, strangely enough, we find similarities in our differences.

It was a pleasure to sit with the editor-in-chief of a provincial newspaper in Zeeland. She too worked in a small society and faced exactly the same day-to-day joys and sorrows that I did in my daily work on top of the Himalayas. Gossip was her newspaper's main competitor too.

I admired a farmer who has taken on the burden of battling the forces of international trade and national import policies to stubbornly prove the sustainability of organic wheat farming. I was impressed by the idealistic fervour of a young man who has convinced 4,000 compatriots to cycle to work, thereby saving the atmosphere from poisonous motor vehicle fumes.

At Amsterdam railway station I watched helplessly, a suitcase in each hand, as a young man grabbed a woman's purse and walked away calmly. Dozens of people just watched. I was inspired by a youth centre in Bylmer, a somewhat dreaded low income group suburb in south east Amsterdam, where a young man ran a fun and healthy recreation centre for misguided youth.

A cattle farmer took me to see his computerized shed where 100 identical cows were fed, milked, analysed, diagnosed, and treated by a computer. I told him that, in Bhutan, we knew our cows by name. He said that he did too, and pointed to a black and white cow: "That one there is 7041."

Of course I had to meet Tim Bodt, alias Sangay, who believes he was a Bhutanese in his past life. He greeted me with a *doma* at Arnhem station.

***

I also realized that the SDA might have come to an end but the in-depth soul searching that it promoted need not. The pursuit of development, widely misinterpreted as purely economic development, needed better goals.

GDP was a broken promise. Despite the staggering economic successes of the industrialised society, and all the wealth of democratic values, I was learning that highly developed countries, including the Netherlands, were beginning to find something missing. Material wealth had not brought the happiness which, perhaps, is our ultimate search.

The co-ordinator of the SDA project, Peter Lammers, had initiated contact with Bhutan, hoping to provoke fresh stimulation. Society as we know it has become unsustainable throughout the world. The climate crisis, which threatens the planet's life as we know it, is not science-fiction but a real dilemma.

Back in 1979 the King of Bhutan was asked by journalists about the kingdom's Gross National Product. His Majesty said that Bhutan was not interested in Gross National Product because Gross National Happiness was more important. Representing a holistic approach to the transformation of society, GNH was soon to inspire other countries as a higher goal for human development.

Gross National Happiness, with its emphasis on preserving the environment, encompasses sustainable development. The Bhutanese people's intuitive belief in the interdependence of all life forms is perhaps a basis for thinking on climate change and ecological balance.

I did not have a clear grasp of the concept of Gross National Happiness. But, like several other Bhutanese and the Dutch proponents of SDA, I was struggling to find it. In that sense we symbolised Bhutan's attempt to define human development and progress.

I visited a 72-year old farmer in a small town in southern Holland. He was proud of the successes of agriculture in Holland. It was a high tech industry that produced thousands of times more than what it did during his youth. The farming community, he pointed out, was a rich one today. Yet his 72-year old wife missed the human warmth of less developed times. "If someone was ill, for example, we would visit each other, with tea and cakes and have long chats," she remembers. "Today we get a pill from an impersonal nurse."

I think I understood what she meant. It was time to go home.